Cover illustration: Aberlemno Stone, Angus

EXPLORING SCOTTISH HISTORY

A DIRECTORY OF RESOURCE CENTRES FOR SCOTTISH LOCAL AND NATIONAL HISTORY IN SCOTLAND

EXPLORING SCOTTISH HISTORY

A DIRECTORY OF RESOURCE CENTRES FOR SCOTTISH LOCAL AND NATIONAL HISTORY IN SCOTLAND

Published by the
Scottish Library Association
and
Scottish Local History Forum
1992

Cataloguing in Publication Data
Exploring Scottish history : a directory of resource centres for Scottish local and
national history in Scotland
I. Title II. Cox, Michael III. Scottish Local History Forum
027.0411025

ISBN 0 900649 79 8

Cover design by Scott Ballantyne

Printed by The Jane Street Printing Company, 4 Jane Street, Edinburgh EH6 5HD

EXPLORING SCOTTISH HISTORY

CONTENTS

INTRODUCTION

Pride in the stewardship of local records, which not so long ago were sometimes left to rot in very damp municipal byways, is reflected in the nearly 240 entries of this directory - archive centres, both new and established institutions, are flourishing. Equally pleasing is the breadth of this guide, which covers subjects from natural history to art, film to literature, geography to sport, genealogy to oral history.

A common denominator among the divers subjects loosely linked by the terms 'local history', the vaguer 'local studies', and the ostensibly unrelated 'family history' and its narrower genealogical base, would appear difficult to find. Their respective practitioners, now aged from eight to eighty, sit shoulder to shoulder in greater and greater numbers in our local history libraries and record offices, apparently sharing neither method nor matter. So, why are they together?

Perhaps what they do share is an outlook. We live in an era that has debunked human grandeur, and have taken or are still taking that displacement of mankind from centre stage to its logical conclusion. We increasingly see ourselves as a minor but integral part of our environment. In the potential chilliness of our new status, we seek warmth from knowing our past. It is significant that the era which destroyed the biblical myths created sociology, with its comforting groups, relationships and processes which have become the tamed rituals of secularisation. A sense of wishing to belong is at the heart of our democratic society, and belonging is a thread which runs through the range of local and family history studies. Our academic disciplines have shifted ground to a study of interactions, and we have converted old institutions to new ends - museums into heritage centres, antiquarian societies into local history societies, archive offices into resource centres.

What advice can one give to the users of this directory, whether new to this range of studies or experienced researchers? The obvious pitfall, given the choice now offered, is the lack of a clearly defined project. Genealogists have the edge here, for they know exactly what they are looking for and will recognise when they have found it. For this reason, the best starting point is the public libraries, with their marvellous miscellanies of books, photographs, maps, newspapers and ephemera. Here one can take stock of the riches of the local environment and the subjects whose different facets can be explored with the help of this directory. Take a town's industry for example. Reports and stories about the establishment of the industry to be found in books or documents in a library can lead on to a study of oral history sources, a search for archive film or photographs from one of the great national collections, an interest in the architectural tradition, geographical studies of location, and so on. The potential for multi-disciplinary and comparative studies is at the heart of success in local research.

Readers consulting this directory should bear in mind that the institutions and organisations featured fall into different categories. Some hold mainly secondary sources - interpretations and explanations from which one derives a context in which to work. These include most libraries, local history societies and museums to some extent. Specialist institutions often bring together both secondary and primary sources on a particular theme. Finally there are the repositories of primary sources which, crucially, do not provide an interpretative framework for the researcher. Institutions in this category include the Scottish Record Office and regional and local archive offices. It should also be noted that many public libraries hold archives of local government and other records as well as their collections of secondary material. The danger for the inexperienced in using primary sources is dilatory wading through a mass of material. It is essential that before going to look at primary source material one has focussed on that relevant, often small amount of research data it is proposed to use and interpret as one's own secondary source. That piece of data is the local historian's equivalent of a genealogist's ancestor.

Most primary sources are definitely not for beginners. The easiest to handle are those now widely available on microfilm or microfiche, such as census enumeration books, valuation rolls, and local newspapers. To these must be added a number of valuable, partially-digested primary sources- halfway between primary and secondary. These include published census reports, the first, second and third statistical accounts, government inquiries, and local authority survey and development reports. These types of records are particularly useful for secondary school and college students undertaking projects, and beginners seeking to get the feel of what has gone in the past in their local area. Their best work, and the published efforts of local and family historians, should be an individual blend produced from the range of rich material listed here, with a telling appreciation of the seemingly trivial detail.

David Moody
Author of 'Scottish local history' (1986), and 'Scottish family history' (1988)

RESOURCE CENTRES FOR SCOTTISH LOCAL AND NATIONAL HISTORY IN SCOTLAND

In 1988 the **Scottish Local History Forum** published a 'Directory of library services for local historians'. This gave outline details of the services offered by Local Authority and University libraries, plus the National Library of Scotland, the National Trust, and Scottish Office libraries. It was felt that this information would be of particular interest to local, family and social historians wishing to find sources of information on many differing aspects of Scottish history.

This modest publication was well received and within eighteen months all copies were sold. Instead of republishing the Directory the Forum's Committee, as a result of suggestions made by members, decided to explore the possibility of publishing a more comprehensive and wide-ranging book. Meetings were held with representatives of the **Scottish Library Association (SLA)**, the **Scottish Records Association (SRA)**, and the **Scottish Museums Federation (SMF)**. They all agreed to support the venture, and the Forum and SLA agreed to fund a joint publication.

Questionnaires were sent out to almost 300 organisations in Scotland who would be likely to hold printed and manuscript material covering a varied range of Scottish history. Replies were eventually received from almost all the organisations by mid-summer, and as a result some 240 entries appear in this Directory. They range from the National Library of Scotland and the Scottish Record Office, local authority and university libraries and archives, smaller specialist libraries and collections, down to small archives currently being developed by local and family history societies. It is inevitable that some resource centres will be missing, either as a result of non-return of a questionnaire or gaps in the knowledge of the participating organisations. The publishers will welcome hearing from any organisation which is 'missing', and wishes to have an entry in a future edition.

Of course, not all archives, records and collections featuring Scottish local and national history are located in Scotland. Collections covering aspects of Scottish history are to be found in such institutions as the British Library, some of the older universities both in Britain and further afield, and archives such as those found in the Vatican and some national libraries in countries which have had connections with Scotland or the Scots. Further resource centres will be found in those countries to which Scots have emigrated over the centuries, and which are familiar to family history researchers. The only non-Scottish archive featured in this publication is the Berwick-upon-Tweed Record Office, which holds material of interest to people who will be researching the past of Berwickshire and the Borders.

Two articles which follow the introductory pages should be read by all researchers who hope to have the results of their labours published. The National Register of Archives (Scotland) (NRA(S)) should always be consulted if a researcher finds that they would wish to look at archives still in private ownership. Researchers will find that the staff not only of the NRA(S) but all the organisations featured in the Directory will be pleased to help genuine researchers, especially those who intend to find out about some aspect of history that has not so far been written about either in the form of a short article or heavy tome!

The recent changes brought about by the Copyright, Designs and Patents Act 1988 should also be borne in mind by researchers, especially in respect of the copying of archival and other material held in archives and libraries. Restrictions should be ascertained at the commencement of any research activities.

Michael Cox - Compiler/Editor
November 1991

THE COLLABORATING ORGANISATIONS

The Scottish Local History Forum was established in 1983. The main aim of the Forum is to bring people together, not only the professional and amateur historians who make contributions to the study of local, family and social history, but also those people who use local historical information (written, oral and visual) in connection with education, tourism and community work, or as part of a modern leisure activity.

The Forum endeavours to act as a catalyst for action, to promote local history broadly defined at both local and national levels, and to help with the establishment and development of groups and societies throughout Scotland. It publishes a Journal three times a year, and organises two Conferences each year which take place at differing venues.

For further information on membership and the Forum's Journal, contact the Hon. Secretary, Scottish Local History Forum, c/o National Museums of Scotland, York Buildings, Queen Street, Edinburgh EH2 1JD.

The Scottish Library Association was founded in 1908 to promote libraries and librarianship in Scotland. Today it has over 2300 members who cover all aspects of library and information work.

The Association publishes a bi-monthly journal 'Scottish libraries', and a wide range of material including posters and a database of local history publications in print. Over the past three years it has promoted Local History Weeks throughout Scotland. In addition it provides training and continuing education courses for members.

Through its members the Association has wide links with schools and resource services, local history groups, universities, and health boards.

Further information on the Association and its publications can be obtained by contacting the Executive Secretary, Scottish Library Association, Motherwell Business Centre, Coursington Road, Motherwell ML1 1PW.

The Scottish Records Association was established in 1977 to arouse public interest in and awareness of historical records relating to Scotland, to provide information on them, and to promote discussion of their custody, preservation, accessibility, and use. Through its twice-yearly conferences, and reports and newsletters, the Association is a forum where the views and needs of custodians of records (owners, archivists, librarians) and users (historians of all kinds, geographers, genealogists, etc.) are aired and discussed.

Local history has featured frequently as a theme in the papers presented to the conferences on a wide range of historical topics, including labour and urban history, genealogy, transport and communications, and the Borders. Sources for local history are listed in the Datasheets which are issued occasionally, containing summaries of the record holdings of local repositories throughout Scotland. They are noted in this Directory under the appropriate archive or library as 'SRA DS' followed by the Datasheet number.

For further information on SRA Datasheets, Conference reports, and membership, write to The Secretary, The Scottish Records Association, c/o The Scottish Record Office, HM General Register House. Edinburgh EH1 3YY.

The Scottish Museums Federation is the independent organisation representing museum staff throughout Scotland. Set up over 50 years ago, the Federation acts as a forum for people in museums to meet together in various parts of the country to discuss issues of topical importance and hear about, and see, recent museum developments. A newsletter is published for members on a regular basis.

The Committee of the Federation is consulted by Government and other agencies on policies affecting museums in Scotland. The Federation is concerned for the well-being of all museums and has contributed to the discussions on such issues as the sale of museum collections and the allocation of funds for archaeological excavations.

NATIONAL REGISTER OF ARCHIVES (SCOTLAND)

The National Register of Archives (Scotland) (NRA(S)), a branch of the Scottish Record Office, has been in existence for over 40 years, giving advice to private owners of historical papers in Scotland, and assisting researchers in gaining access.

Over 3000 reports on collections of papers, some of only a few pages, other extending to hundreds of papers, are available for consultation in the Search Rooms at the General Register House and West Register House (refer to the Directory entry for the Scottish Record Office). An index to the titles of surveys is available, and summaries are published in the Annual Report of the Keeper of the Records of Scotland. Copies of the reports can also be seen at the National Library of Scotland.

In some cases, the reports have been compiled by the National Register of Archives in London, while finding aids compiled by the private owners or their lawyers have been copied. There are also lists produced by local authority and university archivists available for consultation, and researchers should initially refer to the entries for the local authority and university libraries and archives listed in this book for access.

There are partial source lists on a number of topics (such as architecture, art, medicine, science and technology), and use can also be made of the biographical index to major figures created by the Historical Manuscripts Commission in London.

The principal area where the NRA(S) can assist researchers is with their knowledge of records still held by private owners, and how such owners can best be approached if access is required. It should be borne in mind that the existence of a survey does not imply that access will be granted. Permission remains at the discretion of the owner. Researchers must scrupulously observe any restrictions owners may place on publication.

The NRA(S) has set down some 'golden rules' which they ask researchers to observe. They should

1) write to the NRA(S) giving as accurately as possible references to the material they wish to see;
2) as far as possible, read all available background material before a visit is arranged, thereby avoiding repeat visits;
3) give full information on why they wish to consult the papers, the nature and reasons for their particular area of research, and whether they intend to publish or paraphrase the material to be consulted;

4) give maximum advance notice for requests to consult papers in private ownership, and be prepared to be flexible with regard to arrangements for visits;
5) not seek to consult private papers for information which is readily available from public sources (such as census enumerators' schedules and valuation rolls);
6) note that some owners ask for donations to local charities and/or make charges for access;
7) properly acknowledge in any publication assistance given - the Registrar will be able to give advice on this.

COPYRIGHT AND THE LIBRARIAN AND ARCHIVIST

This article covers the copying by a librarian or archivist of 'original literary, dramatic, musical or artistic works'. This definition includes computer programs (considered literary), and maps, drawings, paintings and photographs (considered artistic, irrespective of quality). The amount of material which can be copied will be dependant on 'fair dealing' (see below), interpreted as no more that 5% of a publication, or one journal article from a magazine. The availability and costs of copying vary from organisation to organisation. Most organisations supply price lists on request.

The Copyright, Designs and Patents Act 1988 has important implications for people wishing to copy original material held in libraries, archives and similar depositories, which they wish to use for personal research and/or subsequent publication. **The information given here relates to the copying of material.** Researchers wishing to use material in publications will need to ascertain the restrictions and costs, and discuss their requirements, with the organisation holding the material.

Perpetual copyright no longer exists. Copyright of the material listed above lasts for 50 years from the death of the author or from the end of 1989, whichever is the later. The only exceptions are **Crown Copyright** (which lasts for 125 years from the year in which the work was created) and **copyright in anonymous works** (which runs for 50 years from the year in which the work was made available to the public).

What may be done without infringing copyright? Under Section 43 of the Act, a 'prescribed' library or archive (defined as one which 'makes works in its custody available to the public for the purpose of reference free of charge') may do certain things in relation to original works still in copyright which are literary, dramatic or musical (but not artistic - see below). They must be available for consultation, and not subject to any limitations imposed by a depositor. The library or archive may make copies for conservation or security purposes; and supply a copy of such material to a member of the public provided that (a) it is required for study or research only, (b) only one copy is supplied, (c) it is paid for at a price not less than the cost attributable to its production, and (d) the copyright holder or depositor has not forbidden copying. **It should be emphasised that the wishes of the owner or depositor of a collection are paramount, and are in no way affected by the provisions set out in Section 43.**

Artistic works, which include maps, drawings, paintings and photographs, are not included in Section 43 as outlined above. It is considered, however, that Section 29, relating to fair dealing, will allow the copying of such material for research purposes.

Where material is still in copyright, applicants for photocopies of any sort are required to sign a declaration to the effect that they have not previously been supplied with photocopies of the same material; that they will only use it for private research; and that to the best of their knowledge the copyright owner or depositor has not prohibited copying of the work. **Researchers should always ascertain from librarians and archivists at an early stage in their studies if there are any restrictions regarding the copying of material they wish to consult or use. This is especially true in the case of copying photographs and maps.**

FORM OF ENTRIES IN THE DIRECTORY

A common layout for all entries has been aimed at. The sequence of information is as follows:

Reference number and **name of the organisation and/or resource centre**, together with its **address** and **telephone number**, and where available, its **fax number**.

Name/title of a person or persons to contact for information, with **telephone/extension number if different** from the resource centre's main number.

A brief **general description** of the collection(s), archival, printed and other material to be found at the centre.

The **terms of use** highlight any need to make prior contact and/or arrange an appointment before making a visit to the resource centre. Where **charges** for entrance and/or services are indicated, they are at the 1991 rate.

Hours of opening usually refer to the days and times the resource centre is open to the general public. Enquirers should note that most **Contacts work office hours**, Monday to Friday, although some members of staff of libraries may be available for consultation at other times. **An initial contact by letter is usually preferred.**

The **location** descriptions supplied by the resource centres have been made as brief as possible. Where appropriate, proximity to railway and bus stations, bus routes, and car parking facilities is indicated: distances are given in miles; 'nearby' means that the facility is approximately 100 to 300 yards away; 'near' is used for distances of 300 to 700 yards. **Access for disabled people is noted if available.**

The **primary source material** listed will in most cases only indicate the range of material to be found at the centre. Most of the larger resource centres publish books and/or leaflets and lists giving far more detailed information than it is possible to include in this book.

The **publications** listed are principally those published by the resource centre which will be of direct interest to enquirers. Many centres also have on sale books of interest to readers in their locality, or visitors to the centre.

Reprographics indicate the range of copying and/or reproduction facilities offered by many resource centres. Prices often vary, even between similar centres, so enquirers should always obtain a current pricelist before ordering reproductions.

NOTE: Census Records (Enumerators' Books) are 'closed' (not available to the general public) for 100 years. This means that Enumerators' Books for 1891 can now be seen at the General Register Office for Scotland, while those resource centres with records for 1841 to 1881 will be in the process of adding those for 1891 to their collection.

Many governmental records are 'closed' for 30 years. Government departments will advise enquirers as to which records are affected by these rules. There is a 100 year closure period on Health Board records containing personal information.

Many Regional and District Council and university Archives hold material outwith their geographic catchment areas. This is especially true where the larger photographic collections are concerned. Two examples are the papers of the Collegiate Church of the Isle of Cumbrae c1850-1926, to be found in the Dundee University Archives, and the Glasgow University Archives' Jackson Photographic Collection which covers many areas of Scotland as well as England, Europe and Egypt!

ABBREVIATIONS USED IN THE ENTRIES

b&w	= black and white [photographs]
C	= century, centuries (e.g. 17th and 18th Centuries)
G.P.O.	= General Post Office
IGI	= International Genealogical Index
IGI(BI)	= International Genealogical Index (British Isles)
IGI(GB)	= International Genealogical Index (Great Britain)
IGI(S)	= International Genealogical Index (Scotland)
IGI(SI)	= International Genealogical Index (Scotland & Ireland)
mfiche	= microfiche
mfilm	= microfilm
mform	= microform (microfiche and microfilm)
mins	= minutes
MS	= manuscript(s)
NB	= nota bene [note well]
NLS	= National Library of Scotland
NMR	= National Monuments Record of Scotland
NMS	= National Museums of Scotland
no.	= number
NRA(S)	= National Register of Archives (Scotland)
OPR	= Old Parish (Parochial) Records
OS	= Ordnance Survey
RCAHMS	= Royal Commission on the Ancient and Historical Monuments of Scotland
SRA DS 6/-	= Scottish Records Association Datasheets reference number (see the section on the SRA for further information)
SRO	= Scottish Record Office
x	= extension [telephone]

ACKNOWLEDGEMENTS

The collaborating organisations wish to thank the following people and organisations who made significant contributions towards the publication of this Directory.

The planning and editorial group:
Michael Cox - Scottish Local History Forum
Brian Osborne and Robert Craig - Scottish Library Association
Dr Tristram Clarke - Scottish Records Association
Derek Janes - Scottish Museums Federation.

The organisations whose members of staff supplied advice and contributed articles:
Scottish Record Office and East Lothian Library Service.

The backroom staff of the Scottish Library Association, who undertook the often frustrating task of deciphering the handwriting of many of the questionnaires, and that of the compiler, when inputting information to the database from which the Directory is produced. Programming for the database was carried out by Gordon Dunsire of Napier Polytechnic of Edinburgh, who also formatted and produced the camera-ready copy for the printers.

To all those people who completed the questionnaires and provided such comprehensive summaries of their collections and archives, and to everyone who makes use of the information provided and who it is hoped will eventually add to our knowledge of times past in Scotland.

1   **Aberdeen and N.E. Scotland Family History Society**

152 King Street, ABERDEEN AB2 3BD
Tel.: 0224-646323
Contact: V Murray

Reference library contains mainly NE Scotland source material, but has a significant collection of material on UK, Canada and Australia.

Unrestricted. Search charges: non-members £1 per hour.

Mon-Fri 1000-1600; Sat 1000-1300.

200 yards north of Castlegate; parking nearby; on bus routes; partial disabled access.

Primary source material: OPRs and Census 1841-81 Grampian area; 1851 census for all counties north of Nairn [mfilm]; OPR indexes for all Scottish counties north of Angus, plus Glasgow, Kinross & Clackmannanshire [mfiche]; many transcripts of stones in NE Scotland graveyards in MS & published copies; IGI(World) 1988.

Publications: Genealogical books covering all Scotland, plus some English; exchange journals with most English, Welsh, Irish FHS & many overseas, especially Australasia; The N.E. of Scotland Biographical & Genealogical Record; Publications list.

Photocopies: A3, A4. Mfilm/mfiche prints: A4.

2   **Aberdeen City Archives and Town Clerk's Library**

Town House, ABERDEEN AB9 1AQ
Tel.: 0224-276276 Fax: 0224-644346
Contact: Miss Cripps (City Archivist)

Town Clerk's Library: local history books and pamphlets, Aberdeen and NE Scotland, mainly 19thC, c.2000 items.

Visitors by appointment.

Mon 1030-1230, 1400-1630; Tue-Fri 0930-1230, 1400-1630.

City Archives is part of the City Solicitor's Dept; the Town House is at the east end of Union St. Access by Queen St./Broad St. entrances only; parking near; disabled access.

Primary source material: City Archives: Archives of Royal Burgh of Aberdeen 12thC-, Burgh of Old Aberdeen 17thC-1891, Burgh of Woodside, 19thC; deposited collections include Aberdeen Congregational Churches 1790-1980; Aberdeen Presbytery 1843-1988; Hall Russell Shipbuilders 19th-20thC.

Publications: A4 leaflet.

Photocopies: up to A3. Mfilm prints: A4. Photographic service.

3   **Aberdeen City Arts - Arts and Museums: Aberdeen Art Gallery**

Schoolhill, ABERDEEN AB9 1FQ
Tel.: 0224-646333 Fax: 0224-632133
Contact: Mr John Edwards (Keeper - Science & Maritime History); Ms Judith Stones (Keeper - Archaeology); Ms Francina Irwin (Keeper - Fine Art)

Science & Maritime History Section houses collections of engineering drawings, shipbuilders' drawings, surveyors' sketchbooks; Masters Certificates; ships' documents; passengers' diaries; photographs and paintings of science, engineering industry and maritime subjects.
Archaeology Section holds collections from City of Aberdeen and Grampian Region and associated documentation.
Fine Art Section includes views of Aberdeen, portraits of eminent Aberdonians.

Prior consultation advisable.

Mon-Wed, Fri-Sat 1000-1700; Thu 1000-2000; Sun 1400-1700.

In city centre; parking nearby; bus links; disabled access.

Primary source material: Science & Maritime History Section: Lewis Shipyard, Aberdeen - drawings of ships (incomplete but large collection, 1920s-1960s); Hall Russell Shipyard, Aberdeen - drawings, specification books, ships' documentation for a large number of ships, 1920s-1980s; business papers relating to the granite industry; George Washington Wilson (photographer) archive (see also Aberdeen University Library entry); Davidson & Kay (Chemists) ledgers, prescription books 1890s-1960s.
Archaeology Section: Archives of excavations in City of Aberdeen since 1973, including typescript, plans, photographs.

Publications: Science and Maritime History Section: Lists available. Archaeology Section: A tale of two burghs : the archaeology of Old and New Aberdeen / J.A. Stones. - 1987; Excavations in the medieval burgh of Aberdeen, 1973-1981 / J.C. Murray. - 1983; Three Scottish Carmelite friaries : excavations at Aberdeen, Linlithgow, Perth, 1980-86 / J.A. Stones. - 1989.

Photocopying and photographic services. List of charges available.

4 Aberdeen City Arts - Libraries: Central Library

Rosemount Viaduct, ABERDEEN AB9 1GU
Tel.: 0224-634622 x225 Fax: 0224-641985
Contact: Mrs E Garden

Collection covers the City of Aberdeen and the three counties of Aberdeen, Banff and Kincardine, including 15000+ books, newspapers, maps, photographs and genealogical material.

Mon-Fri 0900-2100; Sat 0900-1700.

In city centre; parking nearby; on bus routes; disabled access.

Primary source material: Newspapers including most published in the city [with the exception of the Aberdeen Journal/Press and Journal, and the Evening Express, all newspapers are printed; the earliest newspaper, the Aberdeen Journal/Press and Journal 1747- is on mfilm]; 2000+ maps 1654- including city plans, railway, harbour, road and canal plans, estate and feuing plans, architectural drawings and OS maps; photographs including 15000+ items 1870s-; special collections of fishing craft, farming life, air raid damage in the city and George Washington Wilson photographs (see also Aberdeen University Library entry); ephemera including theatre programmes, posters and playbills, etc.; OPRs, census returns, voters' & valuation rolls, Aberdeen Post Office directories 1824-1982.

Publications: Leaflet. Copies of booklets, maps, photographs and postcards can be purchased.

Photocopies: A4, A3 or larger (maps only). Mfilm prints: A4. Photographic prints available.

5   **Aberdeen University: Centre for Scottish Studies**

Old Brewery, The University, High Street, ABERDEEN AB9 2UB
Tel.: 0224-272474/272342
Contact: Mr John S Smith (Director)

Visitors by appointment.

1.5 miles north of city centre; parking nearby.

Publications: Selection of booklets on aspects of local history &
historical geography of northern Scotland; annual publication:
Northern Scotland; lists & prices available.

6   **Aberdeen University: Department of Geography**

Elphinstone Road, ABERDEEN AB9 2UF
Tel.: 0224-272328   Fax: 0224-487048
Contact: L McLean (Cartographic Development Officer)
Contact's tel.no.: 0224-272325.

**McDonald Collection of 5000 feu & estate plans, mostly of
Aberdeen and NE Scotland.**

Prior consultation advisable.

Mon-Fri 0900-1200, 1400-1630.

On University campus, 1.5 miles north of city centre; parking.

Photocopies: A3, A4.

7   **Aberdeen University: Library**

Queen Mother Library, Meston Walk, ABERDEEN AB9 2UE
Tel.: 0224-272579   Fax: 0224-487048
**Contact: Mr Colin McLaren (Head of Special Collections,
University Archivist); Ms Myrtle Anderson-Smith (Sub-Librarian);
Mr Iain Beavan (Sub-Librarian)**
Contacts' tel.no.: 0224-272599/8.

**Queen Mother Library has a good general collection of 19th &
20thC historical & topographical material, including an
extensive collection of OS maps and directories.
Department of Special Collections and Archives: The Local
Collection covers all aspects of local studies for Grampian
Region, in 18th, 19th and 20thC books, pamphlets, periodicals,
maps, plans and photographs; of some 3000 MS and archival
collections, the majority relate to the history and culture of the**

North-East; the O'Dell Collection is one of the largest resources in Scotland for Scottish railways; the MacBean Collection comprises about 4000 books, plus articles, pamphlets and prints on the Jacobites; the Simpson Collection is the working library of c.250 books and pamphlets compiled by Dr W Douglas Simpson, an authority on Scottish castellated architecture; the Thomson, Herald, King Collections of pamphlets in almost 1000 volumes were gathered in the 19thC by a local landed gentleman, a local newspaper office and a local printer; the pi and SB Collections of early printed material (pre-1841) include much of Scottish interest.

Prior consultation advisable.

Mon-Fri 0930-1230, 1330-1630.

King's College, with its distinctive crown tower, is on College Bounds, Old Aberdeen, off St. Machar Drive, about 2 miles north of the city centre, on the no.20 bus route; visitors arriving from the south by car should take the ring road (Anderson Drive) and follow signs for the University; parking; disabled access.

Primary source material: Queen Mother Library: historical runs of parliamentary papers, periodicals and record society publications.
Department of Special Collections & Archives:
Local Collection: large collection of pamphlets; 19th-20thC runs of several local and other Scottish newspapers, some on mfilm, notably the unique almost complete run of the Aberdeen Journal (indexed to 1861, later Press and Journal); Aberdeen Almanac from 1774, Aberdeen Directory from 1824; local valuation rolls; all material printed in Aberdeen before 1801, emphasis on University.
MS and Archives: the University's own archives, from 1495; non-archival collections relating to the three constituent Universities; records of local families, estates, institutions and firms.
O'Dell Collection: large collection of plans and sections; timetables; scrapbooks, including MS letters and notes. Some GNSR and LNER archival material.
MacBean Collection: contemporary publications; prints of historical and topographical scenes; 19thC photographs of Scottish topography.
Simpson Collection: 5500 glass lantern slides, mainly Scottish archaeological antiquities. Ms additions to author's own works.
George Washington Wilson Collection: about 40,000 glass photographic negatives, c.1860-1908, of most parts of Scotland, serving the tourist trade, but including much of social and industrial interest (indexed by place and subject) (see also Aberdeen City Arts - Libraries entry).

Publications: Welcome to Aberdeen University Library; Department of Special Collections and Archives; George Washington Wilson Collection.

Photocopies: A3, A4. Mfilm prints: A4. Photographic service for b&w negatives and prints, colour transparencies, mfilming, mounting and print finishing.

8   Abertay Historical Society

c/o Archive Centre, 21 City Square, DUNDEE DD1 3BY
Tel.: 0382-23141 x4494 Fax: 0382-203302
Contact the Hon. Publications Secretary in writing.

Publications: Over 20 on a variety of topics and covering places in the Tay Valley. List and prices on application.

9   Allan Ramsay Library

Leadhills Miners' Reading Institute, Main Street, LEADHILLS ML12 6XP
Contact: The Hon. Secretary.

Over 3000 books including biography, geography, history and theology. Special collection covering mining records, mining tools and minutes from mid 18thC.

Visitors by appointment. Donations welcome.

Wed, Sat-Sun 1400-1600 (May-Sep).

In centre of village; parking nearby.

Primary source material: Book collection, catalogued, including much of the original stock (copies of the catalogue are in the NLS, Edinburgh and the Mitchell Library, Glasgow); MS: Library Society minutes 1821- [MS]; Curling Club minutes 1784-1864 [MS]; Water Committee records 1940-61 (4 books) [MS]; Friendly Society a/c Book 1908-15 [MS]; two hand written catalogues (no date); Gibson Letters 1834-45 and journals and Bargain Books of the Scots Mines Company 1740-1854 (on mfilm in the SRO); 4 boxes of miscellaneous papers (part hand listed); 2 folders of press cuttings, etc.; 4 albums of photographs c1880s- (unlisted).

10   Alloa Museum and Gallery

Speirs Centre, 29 Primrose Street, ALLOA FK10 1JJ
Tel.: 0259-213131 x134
Contact: Ms Jannette Archibald; Mr S Rogers

The Museum houses a collection pertaining to Clackmannanshire's social history.

Prior consultation advisable.

Mon, Wed-Fri 1000-1600; Sat 1000-1230.

In town centre; bus service available to Shillinghill; parking nearby; disabled access.

Primary source material: Postcards, photographs & slides; newspapers; History of Clackmannshire [mfilm]; industrial & commercial documents.

Publications: 'Friends of Alloa Museum' information leaflet; newsletter.

Photocopies: A2, A3, A4.

11   Angus District Libraries and Museums Service: Arbroath Library

Hill Terrace, ARBROATH DD11 1AH
Tel.: 0241-72248
Contact: Mr A Sutherland (Librarian)

Arbroath photographic collection; newspapers and yearbooks.

Mon, Wed 0930-2000; Tue, Thu 0930-1800; Fri-Sat 0930-1700.

Central location; parking nearby; disabled access.

Primary source material: Indexed collection of local photographs; newspaper index, local newspapers [mostly on mfilm]; Arbroath & Forfar News 02/04/1856-28/03/1857, Arbroath Guide 1844-1978, Arbroath Journal 12/01/1839, Arbroath Herald & Advertiser 1889-1988; Arbroath Year Books 1891-1956; lists of people in Montrose Burgh Court Records 1707-1826; 40 oral history interviews.

Photocopies: A3, A4. Mfilm prints: A4. Photographic copying service.

12   **Angus District Libraries and Museums Service: Arbroath Museum**

Signal Tower, ARBROATH DD11 1PU
Tel.: 0241- 75598
Contact: Mrs Margaret King

Collection of maps, prints, drawings, photographs, portraits and local history files.

Prior consultation advisable.

Mon-Sat 1030-1300, 1400-1700 (Apr-Oct); Mon-Sat 1400-1700 (Nov-Mar); Sun 1400-1700 (Jul-Aug).

Former shore base for Bell Rock Lighthouse staff, close to Arbroath Harbour; parking; disabled access (ground floor only).

Primary source material: Arbroath shipping index; Arbroath harbour records; Arbroath trades index 1880-; list of Arbroath burgesses; Shanks Lawnmower archive; Bellrock Lighthouse archive; Arbroath Weavers' minute book 1693-1938 (with gaps); fishing boat index from present day working backwards.

Photocopies: A3, A4. Mfilm prints. Photographic copying.

13   **Angus District Libraries and Museums Service: Archive Department**

Montrose Public Library, 214 High Street, MONTROSE DD10 8PH
Tel.: 0674-73256
Contact: Mrs Fiona Scharlou (Archivist)

The archives contain the burgh and trade records of Arbroath, Brechin, Forfar and Montrose, plus the burgh records of Carnoustie and Kirriemuir. The miscellaneous collection covers a wide range of places and people, and includes diaries, newspaper clippings, society records, sermons, etc. SRS DS 6/9 & 6/10.

Visitors by appointment.

Mon-Fri 0930-1700.

Centre of town; street parking nearby; disabled access.

Primary source material: Burgh records: minute books; protocol books, service of heirs, decreets, etc.; court books; chartularies, charities. Trade records: Arbroath: glovers 1653-1938, hammermen 1844-1938, shoemakers 1741-1937; Brechin: bakers 1622-1880, tailors 1660-1675, shoemakers 1660-1849, weavers 1685-1878; Forfar: tailors 1648-1898, shoemakers 1649-1898, weavers 1685-1878; Montrose: apprentice hammermen 1725-1762. Miscellaneous collection includes diaries of Margaret Forrest Mill 1910-1914; Tarry Mills (Arbroath) Cash book 1803-1823; Brechin Infant School 1835-1858; Weddermain of Pearsie Farm accounts 1833-1856.

Publications: Detailed lists of the records.

Photocopies: A4. Mfilm prints. Photographic copying service.

14   Angus District Libraries and Museums Service: Brechin Library

St Ninian's Square, BRECHIN DD9 7AA
Tel.: 03562-2678
Contact: Mrs A P Robertson (Librarian)

Brechin photographic and newspapers collection with some miscellaneous historical documents of area.

Mon, Wed 0930-2000; Tue, Thu 0930-1800; Fri-Sat 0930-1700.

Central; on-street parking; disabled access.

Primary source material: Indexed collection of local photographs; newspaper index, newspapers mostly on mfilm; Brechin Advertiser 1848-, Brechin & District News 30/10/1952-Jan 1953, Brechin Herald 18/02/1890-12/04/1892; card catalogue of names in: Brechin Burgess Records 1707-1975, Old Wrights' Society of Brechin Membership Book 1801-1836, St James' Lodge of Free Gardeners Register 1806-1836; Commissariot Record of Brechin - Register of Testaments 1576-1800; some local family trees.

Photocopies: A4. Mfilm prints. Photographic copying service.

15   Angus District Libraries and Museums Service: Carnoustie Library

21 High Street, CARNOUSTIE DD7 6AN
Tel.: 0241-59620
Contact: Mr Colin Dakers (Librarian)

Comprehensive collection of printed material about Carnoustie, South Angus and the area in general, plus photographs and newspaper collections.

Mon, Wed 0930-2000; Tue, Thu 0930-1800; Fri-Sat 0930-1700.

Main street; parking; disabled access.

Primary source material: Indexed photographic collection; local newspapers on mfilm: Broughty Ferry Guide, Carnoustie Gazette 1889-1988, Bro'ty Advertiser 1915-1919.

Photocopies: A4. Mfilm prints. Photographic copying service.

16   Angus District Libraries and Museums Service: Forfar Library

50 West High Street, FORFAR DD8 2EG
Tel.: 0307-66071
Contact: Mr I K Neil (Librarian)

Directories, local photograph and newspaper collections, census returns and OPRs, plus the John C. Ewing collection, a comprehensive collection of Scottish material assembled over a period of about 40 years.

Mon, Wed 0930-2000; Tue, Fri 0930-1800; Thu, Sat 0930-1700.

Main street; parking; disabled access.

Primary source material: Indexed collection of local photographs; local newspapers mostly on mfilm: Forfar Dispatch 1912-1988; census returns 1841-1881; OPRs plus index (Angus only); county year books 1812, 1829-46, 1855; Forfar town directories 1855-1939; name indexes to Minutes of Trade Incorporations: 17th-19thC.

Photocopies: A4. Mfilm prints: A4. Photographic copying service.

17   Angus District Libraries and Museums Service: Montrose Public Library

214 High Street, MONTROSE DD10 8PH
Tel.: 0674-73256
Contact: Mr J Doherty (Librarian)

Montrose Year books; local photographs and newspaper collections, plus some burgh records.

Mon, Wed 0930-2000; Tue, Thu 0930-1800; Fri, Sat 0930-1700.

Close to centre of town; street parking nearby; disabled access.

Primary source material: Indexed collection of photographs; mfilm copies of local newspapers: Garden City News (Montrose) 09/05/1935-05/03/1936, Montrose, Arbroath & Brechin Review 17/04/1818-18/10/1839, 1844-47, 1849-75, 1884-1988, Montrose Chronicle 1895-98, Penny Press (Montrose) 1865-67, Scottish Nation (Montrose) 8/5/1923-25/12/1923, Montrose Standard 1844-1970; Montrose Year books 1888-1979; index of Burgh Court Claims 1707-1856; Roll of Provosts, Baillies & Councillors 1296-1888; Montrose craftsmen 1770s-1920s.

Photocopies: A4. Mfilm prints. Photographic copying service.

18   Angus District Libraries and Museums Service: Montrose Museum and Art Gallery

Panmure Place, MONTROSE DD10 8HE
Tel.: 0674-73232
Contact: Mr N K Atkinson

Collection of maps, prints, drawings, photographs, portraits and a range of Montrose records and local history files.

Prior consultation advisable.

Mon-Sat 1030-1300, 1400-1700 (Apr-Oct); Mon-Fri 1400-1700; Sat 1030-1300, 1400-1700 (Nov-Mar).

Close to town centre; parking nearby; disabled access.

Primary source material: Angus Craftsmen, arranged by town; Montrose building and property index, based on 1926 Valuation Roll; Montrose Burgh records, alphabetical index by subject & name; Montrose Chamber Chest, based on J G Low's Inventory; Montrose industry & commerce index, based on the Montrose Yearbooks; Montrose Kirkyards; Montrose obituaries 1884-1930, based on the Montrose Yearbooks; Montrose Old

Kirkyard gravestone inscriptions; Montrose shipping index; Wood's map of Montrose 1822; Burgh Court claims 1707-1820, 1824-1856; Montrose Harbour records 1937-1967.

Photocopies: A3, A4. Mfilm prints. Photographic copying.

19   **Angus District Libraries and Museums Service: William Coull Anderson Library of Genealogy**

Dewar House, Hill Terrace, ARBROATH DD11 1AJ
Tel.: 0241-76221 x240
Contact: Mr Lawrence R Burness (Keeper)

Comprehensive collection of books on genealogical research; books on people, pertaining to their genealogical background; presscuttings; genealogical and family history society journals; photographs of persons and places with genealogical connections; monumental inscription books; burial registers and Fastis.

Visitors by appointment.

Mon-Fri 0900-1200, 1330-1700.

In the District Council offices; local buses near; parking nearby.

Primary source material: Mfilms and photocopies of OPRs for certain Angus parishes; mfilms of 1851, 1861, and 1871 Censuses of many Angus parishes, plus a number of parishes in the counties of Kincardine and Perth; IGI(S), 1988 ed., a large collection of typescript and MS tabulations of family genealogies; transcripts of birth, death and marriage records, census records, Kirk Session records; material covering the families of Burns and Coull.

Publications: Leaflets about the William Coull Anderson Trust and the Library.

Photocopies: A3, A4, B4 and A5.

20   **Angus Folk Museum**

Kirkwynd, Glamis, FORFAR DD8 1RT
Tel.: 0307-84288
Contact: Mrs Valerie McAlister
Contact's tel.no.: 0307-63440.

The Collection contains more than 5000 artifacts. It includes maps and photographs, and a small collection of display books with some data relating to Angus.

Prior consultation advisable. Admission: adult £1.40; child, OAP 70p (1991).

Sun-Sat 1100-1700 (end Apr-end Sep, plus Easter).

Off the Square in Glamis; parking; infrequent bus service; disabled access.

Primary source material: Forfar children's street rhymes and singing games; some letters from emigrants.

Publications: Angus country life; Angus Folk Museum leaflet and companion.

tel. 01369-703214

21 **Argyll & Bute District Archives**   *Manse Brae*

Kilmory, LOCHGILPHEAD PA31 8RT   *01546-602072*
Tel.: 0546-2127 x4120   Fax: 0546-3956
Contact: Mr Murdo MacDonald (Archivist)

Local authority and deposited records; small reference library with finding aids; OS plans.

Prior consultation advisable.

Mon-Thu 0900-1300, 1400-1715; Fri 0900-1300, 1400-1600.

In District Council Offices, Manse Brae; on bus route; parking; disabled access.

Primary source material: Local authority records: Burgh records of Campbeltown 1700-, Dunoon 1868-, Inveraray 1655-, Lochgilphead 1859-, Oban 1817-, Rothesay 1654-, Tobermory 1876-; County Council records of Bute and Argyll 1890-; Parochial Board/Parish Council records 1845-1930, School Board records 1873-1919; Commissioners of Supply records of Argyll 1744-, and Bute 1678-. Deposited records include: Malcolm of Poltalloch from 17thC; Campbell of Kilberry from 17thC; Duncan Colville collection, Campbell of Craignish charters from 16thC; Sproat and Cameron letters (Isle of Mull, 19thC).

Publications: Catalogues/lists available in Archives and NRA(S).

Photocopies: A3, A4.

Council

22   **Argyll & Bute ~~District~~ Library Service: Local Studies Collection**

District Library Headquarters, Hunter Street, Kirn, DUNOON
PA23 8JR   *(01369) 703735*
Tel.: 0369-3214
Contact: Mr W L Scott (Local Studies Librarian)

Comprehensive collection of books relating to the district and its inhabitants; postcard collection; limited range of periodicals and local newspapers; photographic collection.

Prior consultation advisable.

Mon-Thu 0900-1300, 1400-1500; Fri 0900-1300, 1400-1545.

1 mile (approx) from Dunoon pier and 0.75 miles from Hunter's Quay pier; infrequent bus service; limited parking; disabled access (prior contact advised).

Primary source material: Over 2000 (pre-1914) photographs of Campbeltown; other material is located at the District Council's Archive, Lochgilphead (qv).

Publications: Leaflet and 16 reproduction postcards.

Photocopies: up to B4.

23   **Ayrshire Sound Archive**

Craigie College of Education, Beech Grove, AYR KA8 0SR
Tel.: 0292-260321 x265
Contact: Mr John Davies; Ms Avril Goodwin

A collection of interviews with local people.

Visitors by appointment, contact Avril Goodwin; reference free, £2 p.a. if not on General Teaching Council list.

South of Race Course, approach via Craigie Way & Beech Grove by car; parking.

Primary source material: A collection of c.150 cassette tapes, covering all aspects of local history.

Publications: Leaflet.

Microfilm & Records Store, 12 Bankhead Terrace, Sighthill South, EDINBURGH EH11 4DY
Tel.: 031-442 7555 Fax: 031-442 7479
Contact: The Archivists.

Scotland's first bank was established by an Act of the Scots Parliament on 17 July 1695. This Act specified that certain records should be preserved for as long as the bank endured. The archive is both extremely rich and wide-ranging, and contains a wealth of material covering the economic development of Scotland.

Visitors by appointment.

Mon-Fri 0930-1630.

Situated on the industrial estate at Sighthill South, 4 miles west of city centre; buses run to the Bankhead roundabout (10 mins walk); parking nearby.

Primary source material: Bank of Scotland records from 1695: lists of proprietors, records of share transfers, minute books, ledgers, correspondence, journals, banknote registers, maps & plans, salary books, branch records, circulars etc.; extensive holdings for the British Linen Bank from 1746 and Union Bank (previously Glasgow Union Banking Co.) from 1830 until their respective mergers with The Bank of Scotland in 1971 and 1955; other bank archives: Aberdeen Banking Co., Edinburgh Linen Co-Partnery, Edinburgh Stapleary of Yarn, Salton Bleachfield, Caledonian, Central, City of Glasgow, Sir Wm Forbes, Leith, Manchester & Liverpool, Montrose, Northumberland & Durham, Paisley, Perth, Perth United, Ship, Thistle. Mainly MS volumes.

Publications: Two major catalogues: NRA(S) Nos 945 & 1110; The Bank of Scotland 1695-1945 / Chas. Malcolm - 1946; The history of the British Linen Bank / Chas. Malcolm - 1950; History of the Union Bank / Robt. Rait - 1930; A brief history of the Bank of Scotland 1990.

Photocopies: A3, A4.

25   Bank of Scotland: Museum

Head Office, The Mound, EDINBURGH EH1 1YZ
Tel.: 031-243 5467 Fax: 031-243 5546
Contact: The Archivists.

Small museum which tells the story of nearly 300 years of banking in Scotland from 1695.

Visitors by appointment outwith opening hours.

Mon-Fri 0930-1645; Thu 0930-1730 (Jul-Sep).

In city centre; Waverley Rail Station and St Andrews Square Bus Station near; parking nearby; disabled access on prior contact.

Primary source material: A wide collection of Scottish banknotes and forgeries of these notes; early pictures & photographs of the bank and staff; Scottish coins; maps, plans and engravings.

Publications: Leaflets.

26   Barrhead & Neilston Historical Association

Secretary: Mrs I. Hughson, Gowanhill,, Gateside, BARRHEAD G78 1TT
Tel.: 041-880 5797
Contact: Mrs I Hughson (Secretary)

Includes photographs and indexed collection of old postcards of the area.

Visitors by appointment.

Primary source material: Miscellaneous MS papers (details on request).

Publications: Historical walks around Neilston & Uplawmoor; Crofthead Mill - the survivor; Gateside in the 19thC; Local heroes; John Robertson, engineer.

27   BBC Scotland: Library Services

Queen Margaret Drive, GLASGOW G12 8DG
Tel.: 041-330 2880   Fax: 041-334 0614
Contact: Ms Mary Heaney (Manager - Library Services)

BBC Radio Scotland archive broadcasts mainly 1960s- (some dating to 1930s). BBC Scotland Television broadcasts 1958-. NB Representative archival samples from earlier years, not comprehensive coverage.

Visitors by appointment; charges £20 per hour research & playback.

Off Great Western Rd at Botanic Gardens; city bus routes; parking near.

Primary source material: Radio: 78s/vinyl/0.25" audiotape recordings; TV: 35mm and 16mm film; 2"/1"/0.75"/0.5" videotape; programme information: scripts and 'Programme-as-broadcast" sheets,some in hard copy, some on 16mm mfilm.

Radio: playback for all formats available. TV: playback for 16mm film, 1"/0.75"/0.5" videotape. Mforms: 16mm reader printer.

28   Bearsden and Milngavie District Libraries: Local Collection

Brookwood Library, 166 Drymen Road, GLASGOW G61 3RJ
Tel.: 041-942 6811   Fax: 041-943 1119
Contact: Ms Elizabeth Brown
Contact's tel.no.: 041-943 0121.

Local collection comprises books, pamphlets, folders, maps, photographs and postcards.

Mon-Fri 1000-2000; Sat 1000-1700.

Brookwood Library is a few minutes from Bearsden Cross; 10 mins from railway station; bus stop opposite; parking; disabled parking and access.

Primary source material: Milngavie & Bearsden Herald from 1901 [mfilm], partly indexed; Census returns 1841-1881 [mfilm]; OPRs for New Kilpatrick and some other parishes [mfilm]; Glasgow Post Office directories 1818-1978; some Burgh and Town Council minutes; Westerton Garden Suburb Co-operative Society Minutes 1915-1929.

Publications: The Bennie Railplane; A short history of Mains; & Craigend; list of materials relating to the Romans.

Photocopies: A4. Mfilm prints.

29   Bennie Museum

9-11 Mansefield Street, BATHGATE EH48 4HU
Tel.: 0506-634944
Contact: W I Millan (Hon Curator)

A collection of material relating to the Bathgate area.

Prior consultation advisable.

Mon-Sat 1100-1530 (Oct-Mar); 1000-1600 (Apr-Sep).

In centre of Bathgate; bus route and parking near.

Primary source material: A varied selection on schools, World Wars I & II, railways, distillery, brewery, glassworks, church and buildings in the Bathgate area.

30   Berwick-upon-Tweed Record Office

Berwick-upon-Tweed Borough Council Offices, Wallace Green, BERWICK-UPON-TWEED TD15 1ED
Tel.: 0289-330044 x275 Fax: 0289-330540
Contact: Mrs Linda Bankier (Archivist-in-charge)

Record Office houses archives and records mainly relating to North Northumberland and the former borough of Berwick-upon-Tweed; there are some documents and sources relating to Scotland.

Prior consultation advisable.

Wed-Thu 0930-1300, 1400-1700.

In the town centre beside the main council offices; railway station and Marygate bus stop near; parking; disabled access.

Primary source material: Relating to Scotland: Marriages at Coldstream 1793-1797 [transcript]; Eyemouth Methodist Church Minute book of Trustees' meetings, 1897-1910, 1913-1931; some 20thC building plans and sale catalogues for Berwickshire; Proceedings of Berwickshire Naturalist Club, 1842-1891 [printed]; River Tweed Commission assessment rolls or schedule of fisheries in River Tweed and streams running into it,

1908-1924, 1926-1938 [MS]; printed reports and commissions re. salmon fishing in Scotland and River Tweed, mid 19th-20thC; 2nd ed. OS maps of River Tweed, Coldstream to mouth of river; IGI(S) [mfiche].

Photocopies: A3, A4.

31   **Biggar Museum Trust**

Moat Park, BIGGAR ML12 6DT
Tel.: 0899-21050
Contact: Mr Brian Lambie

Local history material includes books, plans, over 8000 photographs [on 35mm negatives], diaries, covering Upper Clyde and Tweed Valleys and parishes surrounding Biggar; also the Albion Motors Archive 1899-c1972.

Prior consultation advisable.

Mon-Sat 1000-1700; Sun 1400-1700 (Easter-Oct); Mon-Fri 1000-1600 (Nov-Easter).

A former church in the centre of Biggar; bus services; parking; disabled access.

Primary source material: Census records 1841-1881 and OPRs for Peeblesshire and local Lanarkshire parishes [mfilm] (list available); shops' & tradesmen's journals and day books; Town Council letter books; newscuttings, c1850- (indexed); photographs - people, events, places, from 1843; George Allan collection of photographs c1937-c1970; architects' plans from 1839; Albion Archive - minute books, plans, manuals, photographs, negatives; Minute books & records of Whipman Society 1808-88; Biggar Gala day, 1907-recent; Horticultural Society, Biggar Dramatic Club, Reading & Recreation Club, etc., Masonic Society records (1726-1800s), local diaries, etc.; Old and New Statistical Accounts for Scotland plus other local history books; transcripts of tombstone inscriptions.

Publications: Horses for hire (Crawford Inn Day Book 1831-55); Diary of J. & A. Noble, Stonemasons, 1783-1800; Biggar St Mary's, a medieval college kirk; Drystone dykers; John Buchan's Tweeddale; Another look at Carnwath; Statement of the wages of the shoemakers of Biggar 1872; George Meikle Kemp, architect of the Scott Monument. Lists available.

8000 photographs on 35mm negatives: details regarding purchase on request.

32   Black Watch Regimental Museum

Balhousie Castle, Hay Street, PERTH PH1 5HS
Contact: Colonel Arbuthnott
Contact's tel.no.: 031-310 8530/8525.

Collection contains material relating to the Black Watch 1725-, including 42nd, 73rd and allied Commonwealth Regiments.

Prior consultation advisable. Search charges by arrangement.

Mon-Fri 1030-1530; Sun (Easter-Sep) 1430-1630.

Hay St runs along the west side of the North Inch; parking nearby; bus route near.

Primary source material: Details contained in the Regimental Documents Survey held by the NRA(S).

33   Borders Region Archive and Local History Centre

Regional Library Headquarters, St Mary's Mill, SELKIRK TD7 5EW
Tel.: 0750-20842 Fax: 0750-22875
Contact: Miss Ros Brown (Archivist)

A large collection of printed material covering the history and way of life in the Borders Region; books by and about local authors including Sir Walter Scott, Andrew Lang and James Hogg; local newspapers, postcards, maps.

Prior consultation advisable. Visitors by appointment to consult mfilm.

Mon-Thu ~~0845-1300, 1400-1700~~; Fri 0845-1300, 1400-1600.

On North Riverside Industrial Area, turn off A7 at Selkirk Glass Visitors Centre; parking; bus route (5 min walk), bus station (15 min steep walk); disabled access.

Primary source material: Pre-1975 records of the County Councils of Berwick, Peebles, Roxburgh and Selkirk, including valuation rolls, minutes of the Turnpike Trusts, County Council minutes, abstracts of accounts, school log books, registers of the poor; deposited collections of local business records, local society records, etc.; OPRs pre-1855 and Census returns 1841-1881 for counties of Roxburgh, Selkirk, Berwick and Peebles [mfilm]; IGI(BI) [mfiche].

Publications: Leaflet available.

Photocopies: A3, A4.

34 Bridge of Weir History Society

c/o Mrs. M. Howison, 7 Horsewood Road, BRIDGE OF WEIR PA11 3BD
Tel.: 0505-690803
Contact: Mrs Margaret Howison; Ms Lorraine Fleming
2nd contact's tel.no.: 0505-612202.

Bridge of Weir (Houston Parish only) 1851 Census return; collection of 125 photographs mostly pre-1914.

Visitors by appointment.

35 Burns Cottage

Alloway, AYR KA7 4PY
Tel.: 0292-41215
Contact: J Manson (Curator)

The Museum houses material relating to the poet Robert Burns.

Prior consultation advisable. Admission £1.50 adults, 75p seniors/children (1991).

Mon-Sat 0900-1900; Sun 1000-1900 (Jun-Aug); Mon-Sat 1000-1700; Sun 1400-1700 (spring & autumn); Mon-Sat 1000-1600 (winter).

In Alloway village, 2 miles south of Ayr; local bus service; parking; disabled access.

Primary source material: A large collection of the poet's MS & correspondence; The Burns Family bible; historical items connected with the poet.

Publications: Leaflets.

36   Bute Museum, Buteshire Natural History Society

Stuart Street, ROTHESAY PA20 0BR
Contact: Mrs Buchanan (Buteshire Natural History Society Librarian)
Contact's tel.no.: 0700-2540.

Local History Archives contain books on the history & natural history of Bute, maps, postcards, photographs, newspaper cuttings, plans and pamphlets.

Visitors by appointment.

Wed 1430-1630 (Library & Archive).

0.25 miles from Rothesay pier opposite Rothesay Castle; parking; disabled access.

Primary source material: Examination Rolls for Rothesay Parish for 1775, 1776, 1814 & 1815; marriage records Nov 1798-Apr 1804, Jan 1811-Dec 1815, Jan 1816-Jan 1822, Apr 1822-Jul 1823; baptismal records Aug 1815-Jun 1822, 1832-1835, plus Kincorth 1821; deeds & papers relating to Parish of Kingarth 1504-1745; deeds & papers relating to Ascog Estate 1507-1752; MS of sermons in Gaelic and English by Rev Archibald McLean 1765-1824, and sermons by Rev J Buchanan, Kinsgarth 1818-1819; MS & reports relating to Robert Thom, water engineer, 1827-47.

Publications: History of Bute; Buteshire Natural History Society's transactions (23 vols).

37   Cameronian Regimental Museum

Mote Hill (off Muir Street), HAMILTON ML3 6BY
Tel.: 0698-428688
Contact: Mr John P McGourty (Assistant Curator-in-Charge)

Collection includes photographs, paintings and drawings depicting the history of the Cameronians (Scottish Rifles) Regiment from its inception in 1689 until its disbandment in 1968. Also features covenanting banners dating from the 17thC.

Prior consultation advisable.

Mon-Sat 1000-1300, 1400-1700.

In the Duke of Hamilton's Old Riding School; parking; approx. 20 min walk from railway station and town centre; disabled access.

Primary source material: NB All records concerning individuals are held by The Army Record Office (post 1900) and The Public Record Office (pre 1900).

Publications: Leaflets. Printed regimental histories.

Photocopy material supplied on request.

38   Carluke Parish Historical Society

79 Hamilton Street, CARLUKE ML8 4HA
Contact: Mrs Christine Warren
Contact's tel.no.: 0555-73462.

Collection comprises miscellaneous papers; over 700 photographs of varying dates; maps of local area including all OS maps for Carluke; artifacts and ephemera (all indexed).

Visitors by appointment. Sat-Sun only.

In town centre; street parking; on bus route; 10 min from railway station.

Primary source material: Records of the Carluke Agricultural Society 1861-1962 [MS].

Publications: Carluke in old picture postcards.

Photocopies: A4.

39   The Cathcart Society

c/o The Secretary, 5 The Elms,, Millholm Road,, GLASGOW G44 3BY
Contact: Ms M C Brown (Secretary)

Publications: Why Cathcart?; Cathcart Old Parish Church 1179-1979; Cathcart and environs (a pictorial reminiscence) 1990; The Cathcart Heritage Trail 1990. All written by Mrs Jean Marshall, former Secretary of the Society.

Unit 6, Burghmuir Industrial Estate, STIRLING FK7 7PY
Tel.: 0786-50745
Contact: Mr G A Dixon (Regional Archivist)

The Archives main holdings are local authority records for, or
inherited by, Central Region and include those inherited by the
Clackmannan, Falkirk and Stirling District Councils; local
church, Justice of the Peace, Customs and Excise records and
over 100 collections of privately deposited records; two long and
one short runs of local newspapers [bound print or mfilm]. SRA
DS 6/3.

Visitors by appointment during Jul-Aug.

Mon-Fri 0900-1230, 1330-1700.

Approx. 100 yards south of Stirling Miner's Welfare Club on
Craigs Roundabout, Stirling; parking.

Primary source material: Stirling Royal Burgh records
1360-1975 [MS and printed]; Police Burgh records for the other
towns in the Region 1850s/1890s-1970s [MS and typescript];
Commissioners of Supply minutes for Stirlingshire 1693-1930,
and for Clackmannanshire 1667-1930 [mainly MS]; County
Council minutes and accounts for both counties 1890-1975 (some
gaps) and for the Region 1975-89; several hundred large-scale
maps, including OS 1858-1970s and smaller-scale maps
c1590-1850; School Board minutes 1873-1919 [MS]; Education
Authorities minutes 1919-30 [printed]; school log books
1863-1988 (with gaps, and 30-years closure) [MS]; various
business, trades union, association, and family (esp. MacGregor
of MacGregor c1314-1921, and Murray of Polmaise, 14th-20thC)
records [MS and printed]; church records of Stirling Presbytery
and constituent Kirk Sessions 1580s-1980s; Registers of Deeds,
Stirling 1620s-1860s; index to burgess admissions Stirling
1700-1938; some burial registers and registers of lairs
1760s-20thC; Stirling Guildry and Incorporated Trades records
15th-20thC [all MS]; testaments: indexes to the pre-1801
Registers of Testaments, Commissariates of Stirling and
Dunblane; sasines abridgements for Stirlingshire 1781-1947,
indexed by person from 1869, by place from 1872; monumental
inscriptions, pre-1855, for East and West Stirlingshire,
Clackmannanshire and SW Perthshire; assorted trade,
commercial and county directories; l9th and 20thC gazetteers;
local histories; West Lothian Hearth Tax returns 1691;
landownership directory for Scotland c1770, printed; collection
of miscellaneous 19th and 20thC photographs; OPRs: St Ninians
Parish, marriages 1688-1854, baptisms 1820-1854, Kippen
Parish, baptisms and marriages 1700-1854, burials 1783-93

[mfilm]; 1841 and 1851 Census enumerators' transcript books for various parishes [mfilm]; newspapers: Falkirk Herald 1845-1886, [mfilm], Stirling Observer 1836-1974 [printed].

Publications: Leaflet describing family history material.

Photocopies: A3, A4.

41   Central Scotland Family History Society

c/o Mrs E. Lindsay, 29 Craiginnan Gardens, DOLLAR FK14 7JA
Tel.: 0259-42585
Contact: Mrs E Lindsay (Secretary)

Collection of material being assembled of interest to family historians in Central Scotland.

Contact the Secretary in writing.

42   Chesters College

2 Chesters Road, BEARSDEN G61 4AG
Tel.: 041-942 8384
Contact: Rev Fr G Donaldson

Extensive collections from Scottish historical & antiquarian societies with many books from the 16thC onwards. Accounts of Scots law & the laws of Scotland, including cases & Acts. Other topics are included in the collection, details on request.

Visitors by appointment.

At the top of Thorn Rd which leads from Bearsden Cross; parking; disabled access.

Primary source material: Histories of the church in Scotland: Roman Catholic and the Church of Scotland; local histories: coverage of Glasgow, Edinburgh & Paisley and others, mainly dating from the 19th and early 20thC.

Photocopies: A2, A3, A4.

43 **Clackmannan District Library Service**

Alloa Library, 26/28 Drysdale Street, ALLOA FK10 1JL
Tel.: 0259-722262 Fax: 0259-219469
Contact: Mr Ian Murray (Reference & Local Studies Librarian)

Collection comprises books, pamphlets, ephemera, slides, photographs, maps, local newspapers and genealogical material.

Mon, Wed-Fri 0930-1900; Tue 0930-1630; Sat 0900-1230.

Local studies collection is at rear of Alloa Library; in town centre; on bus routes; parking nearby; disabled access.

Primary source material: Newspapers [mfilm]: Clackmannanshire Advertiser 1844-1859, Alloa Journal 1854-1972, Alloa Advertiser 1850-1972, Alloa Advertiser & Journal 1972-present, Tillicoultry News 1879-1900, Devon Valley Tribune 1899-1953, Fifeshire Journal 1833-1870; Alloa Circular 1893-1971; Valuation rolls 1959-89; Annual Register for the County of Clackmannan (later County Register) 1874-1912; Alloa Burgh minutes 1899-1972; Clackmannanshire Education Committee minutes 1952-75; Clackmannan District & Central Region minutes, 1975-; miscellaneous archival and MS material; colliery plans & mineral reports; a comprehensive range of OS maps including 1:500 Alloa 1860s.

Publications: Publications list (over 50 items).

Photocopies: A4. Mfilm/mfiche prints.

44 **Clan Donald Centre Library**

Armadale, Ardvasar, Sleat, ISLAND OF SKYE IV45 8RS
Tel.: 04714-389/227 Fax: 04714-275 01471 — 844306
Contact: Ms Maggie Macdonald (Archivist)

A comprehensive reference collection on Scottish history, literature & culture, with particular emphasis on the Highlands & Islands. It has a growing collection of MS & archives, maps, plans, photos, postcards, prints & drawings, and genealogical material.

Admission by day ticket to Centre or with annual library membership (£5). Charges for use of mfilm readers (£1.50 per half hour). Search fees for postal enquiries.

Mon-Fri 0930-1700 (Easter to end of Oct).

1 mile from Armadale pier, the library is at the rear of the Centre's gardens; parking; limited disabled access.

Primary source material: The Macdonald estate papers for Skye & North Uist (mainly 18th & 19thC), and the Glenalladale papers (early 19thC) [MS]; Census enumeration books 1841-81 [mfilm]; OPRs (Skye parishes) [mfilm].

Photocopies: A3, A4.

45   Clydebank District Libraries

Central Library, Dumbarton Road, CLYDEBANK G81 1XH
Tel.: 041-952 8765
Contact: Miss P Malcolm (Information Services Librarian)

The Local History Collection covers Clydebank, particularly shipbuilding and the Singer Sewing Machine Company.

Prior consultation advisable.

Mon-Fri 1000-2000; Sat 1000-1700.

In town centre; limited parking nearby.

Primary source material: Information relating to shipbuilding, the Singer Sewing Machine Company and the Blitz; some MS material; local newspaper [mfiche].

Publications: List available.

Photocopies: A3, A4.

South Lanarkshire Library Service

46   Clydesdale District Libraries: Local History Collection

Lindsay Institute, 16 Hope Street, LANARK ML11 7LZ
Tel.: 0555-61331   01555 661144
Contact: Mr Gordon Kane (Principal Officer)

Collection comprises 1850 books, documents, scrapbooks, newspapers; 160 maps and plans 1850-; 300 photographs of events and places plus 600 postcards; census and OPRs, 19thC; local authority records. SRA DS 6/25.

Mon-Wed, Fri 1000-1930; Thu, Sat 1000-1700.

Near town centre; railway and bus stations near; parking nearby; disabled access.   (Isobel Walker)

Local History: Reference Services Manager,
Hamilton Central Library, 98 Cadzow St,
Hamilton, ML3 6HE. Tel (01698) 452463

39

Primary source material: Carluke & Lanark Gazette 1954-; Carluke & Lanark Advertiser 1982-.

Publications: Old Clydesdale in photographs.

Photocopies: A4.

47   The Cockburn Association

Trunk's Close,, 55 High Street, EDINBURGH EH1 1SR
Tel.: 031-557 8686   Fax: 031-557 9387
Contact: The Secretary.

Cockburn Association Annual Reports 1895-1970 and Newsletters 1971 to date, covering planning/conservation issues in Edinburgh. NB They can be seen at the NLS & Central Library in Edinburgh.

Visitors by appointment.

Mon-Fri 0930-1730.

In Trunk's Close off the High St. Waverley Station nearby, St Andrews Square Bus Station near; parking nearby.

Primary source material: Cockburn Association minute books.

Photocopies: A3, A4.

48   Colinton Local History Society Library

c/o The Secretary, 32 Bonaly Terrace, EDINBURGH EH13 0EL
Tel.: 031-441 1412
Contact: The Secretary.

The Local History Library comprises over 30 books on local history topics plus a collection of photographs and slides of local interest.

Visitors by appointment.

Mon-Fri afternoons.

In executive committee member's house; street parking; local bus service.

Primary source material: Uncatalogued collection of photographs, slides of local interest.

Publications: List available from The Secretary.

49   The Corstorphine Trust

199a St John's Road, EDINBURGH EH12 7UU
Tel.: [Moving to new address, 1992]
Contact: The Curator.

Collection of photographs & archives.

Prior consultation advisable.

Sat 1000-1200.

On main road; no immediate parking; on bus routes.

Primary source material: Corstorphine Estate documents; Forrester and other local families photographs; local history memorabilia.

Publications: Leaflet available.

50   Cromarty Courthouse

Church Street, CROMARTY IV11 8XA
Tel.: 03817-418   Fax: 03817-418
Contact: Mr David Alston (Curator)

The museum maintains a series of public access files on aspects of the history of Cromarty, with an emphasis on the late 18thC.

Prior consultation advisable. Admission charge.

Mon-Fri 1000-1700.

In town centre; on street parking; bus service.

Primary source material: Court papers and papers relating to County & Burgh administration, mostly 19thC [MS].

Publications: Leaflets available.

Photocopies: A3, A4.

51   **Cumbernauld & Kilsyth District Library: Central Library**

8 Allander Walk, CUMBERNAULD G67 1EE
Tel.: 0236-725664
Contact: Mr J Alexander (Depute District Librarian)

Local collection comprises books, photographs, maps, newspapers, reports and minutes of local authority and community groups in Cumbernauld, Kilsyth and the former counties; also fiction works by local authors. NB Some material relating specifically to Kilsyth housed at Kilsyth Library, Burngreen, Kilsyth, tel.: 0236-823147.

Prior consultation advisable.

Mon-Tue, Thu-Fri 1000-2100; Wed 0900-1700.

The local collection is housed in Cumbernauld Central Library on Level 3 of the Cumbernauld Centre; bus services at Centre; parking; disabled access.

Primary source material: Census enumeration books for Cumbernauld & Kilsyth 1851-1881 [mfilm]; OPRs for Cumbernauld 1688-1854, and Kilsyth 1619-1854 [mfilm]; newspapers Cumbernauld News 1982-1990 & Kilsyth Chronicle 1986-1990 [mfilm]; minutes of Cumbernauld Subscription Library c1820, Cumbernauld Southern District Debating Society c1932 [MS].

Publications: Leaflets & publications of local historical interest.

Photocopies: A3, A4.

52   **Cumnock and Doon Valley District Library: Library Headquarters**

District Council Offices, Lugar, CUMNOCK KA18 3JQ
Tel.: 0290-22111 x317   Fax: 0290-22461
Contact: Mr John Laurenson

Local History Collection houses a comprehensive collection of books on people, places and events in Cumnock and Doon Valley District and Ayrshire, plus articles, journals, maps, photographs, postcards, oral history cassettes, videos and ephemera.

Visitors by appointment.

Mon-Fri 0900-1630.

One mile NE of Cumnock on the A70; disabled access by prior arrangement.

Primary source material: Census enumeration books 1841-1881 [mfilm]; OPRs 1650-1854 [mfilm]; Register of the Great Seal of Scotland 1306-1668; IGI(S,I) [mfilm]; pre-1918 gravestone inscriptions for Cumnock and Doon Valley District; Ayr Advertiser 1834-1939 (gaps), 1952- (gaps); Cumnock Chronicle 1960-; collection of miscellaneous archival and MS records.

Publications: Local history leaflet available.

Photocopies: A3, A4. Photographic reproduction available on request.

53   **Cunninghame District Council Museums Service: North Ayrshire Museum**

Manse Street, SALTCOATS KA21 5AA
Tel.: 0294-64174
Contact: Mrs Linda Miller

Museum houses a collection of both original and photocopied material from the North Ayrshire area, particularly Stevenston, Saltcoats and Ardrossan and some family papers from the Beith area, and includes maps, plans and photographs.

Prior consultation advisable.

Mon-Tue, Thu-Sat 1000-1300, 1400-1700 (Jun-Sep); Tue, Thu-Sat 1000-1300, 1400-1700 (Oct-May).

The museum is near the town centre by the Post Office; bus service at front door; limited parking nearby; disabled access.

Primary source material: Papers of the Hume, Reid, Shedden, Cochrane Patrick and Allen families from the Beith area 18thC-; photographs of the three towns area 1900-; local business papers pertaining to the three towns and central Cunninghame; large collection of lantern slides covering the Clyde coast area and its shipping.

Publications: Stevenston, kernal of Cunninghame / J. Clements; Things that befell in Ayrshire / J. Clements; Saltcoats: a brief history / Saltcoats Community Council; Ardrossan shipyards 1825-1923 / Dr. C. Levy & Ardrossan Local History Group; Ardrossan harbour 1805-1970 / Dr. C. Levy & Ardrossan Local History Group; Kilwinning Abbey / Sister D. Savio; Knight and the umbrella / Ian Anstruther.

Photocopies: A3, A4. Copies of photographs up to 8x10", larger sizes by special arrangement.

54   Cunninghame District Library Service: Library Headquarters

Princes Street, ARDROSSAN KA22 8BT
Tel.: 0294-69137 x36 Fax: 0294-604236
Contact: Mrs Judith Davenport (Local Studies Librarian)

Local collection contains past and present material concerning Scotland, with particular emphasis on Cunninghame District, North Ayrshire, including books, pamphlets, photographs, maps & plans, newspapers, monumental inscriptions, and ephemera.

Visitors by appointment.

Mon-Fri 0930-1645.

In town centre; parking at rear (off Glasgow St); Ardrossan Town railway station & bus services near; disabled access.

Primary source material: Census enumeration books 1841-1881 and OPRs for Cunninghame District [mfilm]; archives include valuation rolls, council minutes, poor relief and licensing court records, charities ledgers, 'invasion' committee records, letter books, etc.; cemetery records for Kilbirnie, Kilwinning, Largs, Millport & West Kilbride; Auchenharvie Papers relate to Saltcoats area covering local mining operations, land transactions, letters, chiefly during 18th & 19thC [MS, photocopies available for consultation].

Publications: Leaflet available.

Photocopies: A3, A4. Mfilm prints: A4, B5. Limited collection of prints from photographs available.

55   **David Livingstone Centre**

Station Road, BLANTYRE G72 9BT
Tel.: 0698-823140
Contact: Mr Geoffrey Peter Smith; Mr John Moore

A comprehensive collection of printed material on David Livingstone; plus a social history collection reflecting the history of the building and of the Blantyre area.

Prior consultation advisable.

Mon-Sat 1000-1800; Sun 1400-1800.

The Centre is signposted from Blantyre Main St; parking; disabled access.

Primary source material: Books & notebooks belonging to or written by David Livingstone, including notebooks 1871-74, original letters 1846-74.

Publications: David Livingstone Centre leaflet.

Photographic services are contracted out £30 reproduction fee for publishers.

56   **Dollar Museum**

East Burnside, DOLLAR FK14 7AX
Contact: Mrs J Carolan (Hon Curator); Mr C Baillie
Contacts' tel.nos.: 0259-42895/42315.

Collection contains books, journals, maps, photographs, postcards and miscellaneous papers relating to people, places and events in Dollar and neighbourhood.

Visitors by appointment, times and charges on application.

The museum will move to new premises at the top of East Burnside in Spring 1992; bus route and parking near. NB Disabled access with disabled parking at the new museum only.

Primary source material: Dollar Magazine 1902-; published 19thC reminiscences; minute books of societies and clubs; early guide books, facsimiles of 18th & 19thC maps; photocopies of some early Dollar Academy archival material, and local cemetery inscriptions.

57   Drymen and District Local History Society

c/o Drymen Library, The Square, DRYMEN G63 0BX
Tel.: 0360-60751   Fax: 0360-60751
Contact: Mrs Alison Brown (Community Librarian)

Local history information of the area. Pack available for reference by school & university students.

Mon, Fri 0930-1300, 1400-1700; Tue, Thu 0930-1300, 1400-1900; Sat 0900-1300.

In the centre of Drymen; parking to rear; on bus route.

Primary source material: Collection is small and consists of cuttings; photocopies of local material including maps (Drymen and Buchanan); a few monographs, slides and prints.

Publications: Drymen and Buchanan in old photographs. - 1988; Strathendrick in old photographs / Mary B. Bruce & Alison Brown. - 1990.

Photocopies: A4, B4.

58   Dumbarton District Libraries: Local Studies Collection

Dumbarton Library, Strathleven Place, DUMBARTON G82 1BD
Tel.: 0389-63129
Contact: Mr Graham Hopner (Local Studies Librarian); Mr Arthur Jones (Local Studies Librarian); Ms Bannister (Helensburgh Collection Librarian)
Contact's tel.no.: 0436-74626 (Helensburgh Collection Librarian).

The Local Studies Collection houses material relating to the people, places, events, industries, pastimes, etc. connected with the District, including c1000 books, 3 cabinets of cuttings, newspapers 1851-, c12000 photographs, c2500 slides, c1000 maps and MS and printed archives (space equivalent of 3,000 volumes from 1424). SRA DS 6/20.

Prior consultation advisable.

Mon-Tue, Thu 1000-2000; Wed, Fri-Sat 1000-1700.

In town centre; Dumbarton Central railway station nearby; on bus route; free parking; disabled access.

Primary source material: Census enumeration books 1841-81 for County of Dumbartonshire [MS, mform]; OPRs for Dumbartonshire and West Stirlingshire 1619-1854 [MS, mform]; Dumbarton & Lennox Heralds 1851- [printed, mform]; Helensburgh & Gareloch Times 1880-1980 [printed, mform]; Dumbartonshire Valuation Rolls 1864- (many gaps) [MS, printed]; Dumbarton Town Council Minutes 1578/9-1975 (C17 gaps) [MS, printed]; Helensburgh Town Council Minutes 1807-1975 [MS, printed]; County Council of Dumbarton Minutes 1895-1975 [printed]; District & Regional Council Minutes 1975- [printed]; Poor relief records of the District 1847-1962 [MS, printed]; Dumbartonshire Directories 1864- (gaps); Sasines for Dumbarton and Argyllshire 1617-1780 persons index [printed]; Testaments for Scotland 1514-1800 persons index [printed].

Publications: Lennox links (of interest to family historians); Cardross: the village in days gone by. - 1985; Discovering Dumbarton District. - 1981; Helensburgh and Garelochside in old pictures. - 1984; Dumbarton at weekend play. - 1981; Lennox lore. - 1987; Dumbarton past and present. - 1989; The Lennox album: Transport. - 1982; leaflet available.

Photocopies: A3, A4. Mfilm/mfiche prints. Prints of photographs available.

59 Dumfries and Galloway Family History Society

c/o Mrs M Robinson, Dykenook, Colvend, DALBEATTIE DG5 4QA
Tel.: 0556-63278
Contact: Mrs Margaret Robinson (Publications Exchange Secretary)

A small collection of local and family history books, including those of other groups, for consultation at meetings.

Prior consultation advisable (by letter initially). Books are available on request or borrowed at Society meetings.

Publications: Newsletters.

Crichton Royal Museum, Easterbrook Hall, Crichton Royal
Hospital, Bankend Road, DUMFRIES DG1 4TG
Tel.: 0387-55301 x2360
Contact: Mrs Morag Williams

**The Archives contain material relating to hospitals in SW
Scotland from the 1770's.**

*Prior consultation advisable (not on Mondays). Visitors by
appointment (Tue-Fri during office hours).*

Thu-Fri 1330-1630 (all year); Sat 1330-1630 (Easter-Oct).

On the south side of town; parking; disabled access.

**Primary source material: Dumfries & Galloway Royal Infirmary
Minute books (2 vols missing), annual reports, cash books,
ledgers, letter books, staff registers 1777-; Crichton Royal
Hospital Crichton Trust documents 1823-, Minute books 1839-,
annual reports, case notes 1839-, registers of admission,
restraint and seclusion, accident, and death, obligants books,
Sheriff's warrants, staff registers; Cottage hospital material
relating to Stranraer, Kirkcudbright, Castle Douglas, Moffat,
Langholm including minutes, annual reports (incomplete), some
letter books, patients registers; infectious diseases hospitals
material including patient registers for Thornhill, Castle
Douglas, Newton Stewart; variety of photographic material;
hospital plans; Area Health Board minutes; oral archive being
attempted. [Material mainly MS; 20thC Minutes for DGRI &
CRH printed; annual reports printed].**

Photocopies: A3, A4.

**61 Dumfries and Galloway Regional Library Service: Local History
Studies Collection**

Ewart Library, Catherine Street, DUMFRIES DG1 1JB
Tel.: 0387-53820 x4285 Fax: 0387-60294
Contact: Mrs Ruth Airley; Mr Graham Roberts

**The Collection contains material relating to Dumfries and
Galloway, including books, pamphlets, maps, plans,
photographs, ephemera, archives and genealogical material.
SRA DS 6/7.**

*Prior consultation advisable. Search charges by letter: £5 +
charges for copies.*

Mon-Wed, Fri 1000-1930; Thu, Sat 1000-1700.

Near town centre, just off the Edinburgh Rd (A701); parking nearby; on bus route; disabled access.

Primary source material: Census for Dumfries and Galloway 1851 [mfiche]; valuation rolls: Dumfriesshire 1862-, Kirkcudbrightshire 1844- (with gaps), Wigtownshire 1904- (with gaps), Dumfries Burgh 1879-1975 (with gaps); Register of Sasines: index 1617-1780; local newspapers [many held on mfiche]; indexes to Dumfries and Galloway Standard and forerunners 1777-1930, and Wigtown Free Press 1843-1925; extensive archives collection including some local authority material.

Publications: For reference: Genealogical guide; Archives guide; Printed ephemera guide; Introduction to 1851 Census; Introduction to International Genealogical Index.
For sale: Posters of old Dumfries (includes Dancing Bear c1908); Historical walk around Lockerbie; Indexes to the Wigtown Free Press; and others.

Photocopies: A3, A4. Prints from mfiche. Copies of photographs from the collection.

62   Dumfries Archive Centre

33 Burns Street, DUMFRIES DG1 2PS
Tel.: 0387-69254
Contact: Miss Marion M Stewart (Archivist)

Collection of documents covering life and administration of Dumfries Burgh mid 15thC-, plus family, business & society records relating to the rest of Dumfriesshire, parts of Kirkcudbrightshire and a little of Wigtownshire. There are also mfilms of local interest records held elsewhere. Small library of reference and local history books and pamphlets.

Visitors by appointment.

Tue-Wed, Fri 0900-1300, 1400-1700; Thu 1800-2100.

In town centre and opposite Robert Burns' house; 10 mins walk from bus station, 15 mins from railway station; parking nearby.

Primary source material: Council minutes 1643-; Petitions 1655-1833; Police Commissioners' records 1811-1949; Railway, Gas, Waterworks, Hospital and Bridge Committee minutes 1850-1929; Parochial Board records 1839-1928; Town Clerks' letter books 1787-1966; Ale, Brokers, Cinema, Hackney

carriage, Motor vehicle and Publicans Registers of Licence applications 1718-1974; Services of Heir Registers 1751-1844; Special Constables Registers 1839-62; Burgh Court books 1506-89; Burgh Court papers 1506-1893; Dean of Guild records 1777-1964; Porteus Rolls 1679-1866; Court Diet books 1658-1832; Jail books 1721-1839; Treasurers' accounts 1633- ; Assessed taxes 1813-65; church seat rentals 1774-1858; Feu Rolls 1674-1825; Police Taxes 1795-1887; shipping, bridge, etc. dues 1756-1802; Stent Rolls 1649, 1718-1839; voting records 1783-1961; Assessment Rolls (various) 1863-1975; many collections of local clubs, businesses & families c.1500-1950 [all MS]; Census returns for Dumfriesshire, Kirkcudbrightshire & Wigtownshire parishes 1841-1871; OPRs for Dumfriesshire & Kirkcudbrightshire [mfilm].

Publications: Information sheets & source lists are available on types and details of records. They include Official & Court records; valuation, taxation & voting records; shipping; church records; health records; poor & welfare; trade & business; transport; military; crime & law; and for genealogists. Small charge made for these. Booklet: Ancestor hunting in Dumfries Archive Centre; Index/Synopsis of Council minutes (c250p) 1730-40 (volumes to follow covering 10 year periods); person indexes to 1851 Census returns (published jointly with Dumfries & Galloway Family History Society.

Photocopies: A3, A4.

63   Dumfries Museum

The Observatory, DUMFRIES DG2 7SW
Tel.: 0387-53374   Fax: 0387-67225
Contact: S R Ratchford

Small collection of books of local interest, some 18th, but most 19th & 20thC; journals & books of Scottish interest including archaeology, social & natural history, literature, numismatics, etc.

Prior consultation advisable.

Mon-Sat 1000-1300, 1400-1700; Sun 1400-1700 (closed Sun-Mon Oct-Mar).

In Church St (west bank of river); parking; railway station 0.75 miles; Whitesands bus station 10 mins; disabled access.

Primary source material: The diaries of William Grierson.

Publications: Almost 100 leaflets on a wide range of topics, list available.

Photocopies: A3, A4; Photographs: 10x8".

64   **Dunblane Cathedral Museum**

The Square, DUNBLANE FK15 0JN
Tel.: 0786-824254
Contact: Mr J G Lindsay

The collection includes artefacts, displays, documents, photographs, prints, pictures & archives concerning the Cathedral; an unique collection of over 6000 communion tokens; the library contains mainly local & church history plus Proceedings of the Society of Antiquaries of Scotland 1882-1957, and Bulletin of John Rylands Library 1950-1971.

Prior consultation advisable. Visitors by appointment (outwith opening times).

Mon-Sat 1030-1230, 1430-1630 (end of May-beginning of Oct).

Centre of town, opposite Cathedral; train & bus services, parking nearby; partial disabled access.

Primary source material: Documents, account books, minute books, plans re Cathedral restoration.

Publications: Journal of the Society of Friends of Dunblane Cathedral. - 1930-.

65   **Dundee District Archive and Record Centre**

Administration Division, 21 City Square, DUNDEE DD1 3BY
Tel.: 0382-23141 x4494   Fax: 0382-203302
Contact: The Archivist.

The Centre acts on an agency basis for Tayside Region. The Archives collection comprises records of the City of Dundee District Council & its antecedents 1327-; records of Tayside Regional Council and its antecedents (Perth & Kinross County Council and Forfarshire/Angus County Council) 1718-; retransmited records from the Scottish Record Office. SRA DS 6/1 & 6/28.

Prior consultation advisable. Visitors by appointment.

Mon-Fri 0915-1300, 1400-1645.

City centre; short term parking at Tay Rd Bridge; long term parking at railway station; access by 14 City Square or 1 Shore Terrace.

Primary source material: City of Dundee: Burgh Court Books 1520-1898; Registers of Deeds 1626-1908; Council Minute & Account Books 1553/1586-1983; Shipping Registers 1580-1713; education records c1864-1985; infrastructure records 1870-1966; Justices of the Peace records 1894-1975; Register of Sasines 1639-1812; Protocol Books 1571-1608; Broughty Ferry Police Commissioners/Town Council Minutes 1877-1913; Monifieth Burgh Commissioners/Town Council Minutes 1895-1925.

Angus, Forfarshire and Perth and Kinross County Council records: Commissioners of Supply and Highway Authorities minutes 18th-20thC; County Council Minutes 1890-1975; education records 1864-1985; Parochial Board/Parish Council Records 1845-1930; Lieutenancy records 1797-1893/1801-1925; Freeholders records 18th-19thC; Montrose Bridge Commissioners/Joint Bridge Committee 1792-1933; Justices of the Peace records 1736-1977/1791-1974 (NB most Perth County records have been retained by the Archivist, Perth & Kinross District Council, Sandeman Library, Perth).

Family and estate papers: Balgay & Logie Estate (Angus) 1495-1962; Ballindean Estate (Perth) 1652-1968; Earls of Camperdown 1830-1890; Dr Thomas Dick (Broughty Ferry) 1782-1857; Geekie Family (Keillor) 1646-1850; Grange Estate (Monifieth) 1625-1767; Lundie Estate (Angus) 1465-1963; Northesk Muniments 1247-1922; Snaigow Estate (Perth) 1606-1962; Strathmartine Estate 1537-1889; Wedderburn of Pearsie 1483-1918; Wharncliffe Papers 1670-1929.

Business Records: Bell & Sime, timber merchants 1900-1980; Dundee, Perth & London Shipping Co. 1826-1960; Halket & Adam, Dundee ropeworks 1926-1968; McGregor & Balfour, shuttlemakers & millfurnishers 1900-1932; Robb Caledon, shipbuilders 1872-1980; Jas Scott & Sons, spinners & jute mfrs. 1861-1969; Victoria Spinning Co. 1893-1978; David Winter & Son, booksellers & publishers 1858-1951.

Trades Records: maltmen 1653-1871; masons 1659-1960; slaters 1684-1976; tailors 1556-1920; Three United 1741-1934; weavers 1557-1951; wrights 1691-1915; Guildry Incorporation 1570-1970.

Trade Unions: engineering 1920-1970; boilermakers 1868-1981; jute & flax 1906-1966; railway clerks 1901-1987; bakers & confectioners 1921-1952; Seamen Fraternity 1652-1978.

Church Records: Baptist, Congregational, Episcopal, Methodist & Unitarian, mostly 19th & 20thC (Methodist from 1771).

Other records: Dundee & Tayside Chamber of Commerce 1819-1960; Dundee Port Authority 1814-1986; schools; societies; institutions; utilities (mostly from end of 19thC).

Publications: List giving outline details.

Photocopies: A4.

Central Library, The Wellgate, DUNDEE DD1 1DB
Tel.: 0382-23141 x4377 Fax: 0382-201117
Contact: Mrs Linda McGill

Collection covers Dundee, Tayside & North East Fife, including 17000 books; newspapers 1803-; 2000 maps & plans; photographs; 25000 items of ephemera, including posters; significant MS collections.

Prior consultation advisable.

Mon-Tue, Fri-Sat 0930-1700; Wed-Thu 0930-1900.

In city centre; in Wellgate Centre; parking; bus routes nearby; railway station 0.5 miles; disabled access.

Primary source material: Mary Slessor collection, chiefly letters [MS], also books & recordings; William McGonagall collection, letters [MS], poems, autobiography, plays and broadsheets. Whaling: small collection of logbooks, including the illustrated 'Camperdown' log [some logs are available on mfilm]. Tay Rail Bridges: the largest extant collection of source material; the MS register of articles found after the disaster is among the more valuable items. Newspapers 1803- and indexed cuttings 1918- [many newspapers have been mfilmed; advance notice of 24 hours is required for hard copy newspapers]. The photographic collection of Alexander Wilson and the thematic Dundee Photographic Survey portray Dundee from 1870-1900 and 1900-1916 respectively. More recent photographs are also available and a 1991 Dundee (Octocentenary) Photographic Survey is in preparation. Poster Collection from 1830, rich in political & theatrical items. The A C Lamb ephemera collection (550 boxes), 19thC printed & MS items. The genealogical collection includes Dundee directories; IGI; monumental inscriptions; obituaries; OPRs; Census returns; electoral & valuation rolls [variously mfilm, fiche & hard copy].

Publications: Genealogical & family history leaflets; Local History Index list (these include ephemera, maps, photographs, shipping, graveyard, trades council, etc.). Handouts are provided for the guidance of researchers.

Photographic prints are supplied to order. Photocopies. Mfilm/mfiche prints. Reproduction to fiche.

67 Dundee University Archive Department

University of Dundee, DUNDEE DD1 4HN
Tel.: 0382-23181 x4095 Fax: 0382-29190
Contact: Ms Joan Auld

An extensive collection of MS, archives & maps relating to Dundee, Tayside & Fife. SRA DS 6/26.

Visitors by appointment.

Mon-Fri 0900-1700.

In Tower Building basement; parking adjacent; disabled access.

Primary source material: University archives: records of the university 1967-; University College and Queens College c1875-1966; Dundee Medical School (University of St Andrews) c1887-1966.
Major MS collections: records of local textile industry and its links with India and Pakistan 1820-1948; engineering c1840-1978; records of Dundee hospitals, including the Dental Hospital, local medical associations 1864-1927; Dundee Medical Library 1880-1903; R.C. Buist collection, history of medicine in Angus 16thC-; papers of R.C. Alexander c1899-1950; medical photographs c1917-1941; Glassite church sermons and correspondence 1728-1885; papers of the College and Collegiate Church of the Holy Spirit, Isle of Cumbrae c1850-1926; MS and correspondence of Thomas Campbell, poet 1797-1854; papers of Alexander Mackenzie c1896-1936, Alexander Scott 1851-1935, Sir Robert Robertson 1894-1949, A D Walsh c1930-1970; records of Dundee Stock Exchange Association 1876-1964; John P. Ingram shipping notebooks 1767-1980; papers of Wilson family; papers relating to James Ballantyre Hannay, diamond research and family affairs 1842-1987; Brechin Diocesan Library MS: correspondence of Bishop Alexander Penrose Forbes 1844-74; transcripts of episcopal registers c1681-1890; records of Diocese of Brechin c1744-1904; Diary and commonplace book of William Drummond of Hawthornden 1606-1619.
Non-MS material: Thornton collection and others, maps and plans [some MS], particularly Dundee and Angus and railway plans c1770-1960; technical drawings c1850-1960; George H. Bell collection of photographs of eminent visitors to the University of Dundee plus miscellaneous photographs, both local & Scotland.

Publications: Archives checklist covers over 100 MS collections.

Photocopies: A3, A4. Prints from mfilm.

68   Dundee University Library: Local History Collection

Main Library, University of Dundee, DUNDEE DD1 4HN
Tel.: 0382-23181 x4084/4086   Fax: 0382-29190
Contact: Mr Michael Shafe (Deputy Librarian); Mr Alan Grant

The Kinnear Local Collection.

Visitors by appointment.

Mon-Fri 0900-1700.

Main Library is in Peters Lane, off Smalls Wynd in Campus
Centre; parking in Park Place (South); buses nearby; bus & railway
stations within walking distance; disabled access.

**Primary source material: The Kinnear Local Collection: 4000
vols on Tayside & Fife (in process of being catalogued). There
is an online author/keyword short catalogue available.**

Photocopies: all sizes. Prints from mfilm.

69   Dunfermline District Libraries: Local History Library

Central Library, Abbot Street, DUNFERMLINE KY12 7NW
Tel.: 0383-723661
*Contact: Mr C Neale (Senior Reference Librarian); Mrs M Stewart
(Local History Librarian)*

**Local history collection developed from the Dr Erskine
Beveridge donation of 60 years ago. It houses books on people,
places, events and industries in Dunfermline and West Fife plus
articles, journals, maps, plans, photographs and ephemera.
Special collections include the George Reid Collection and the
Murison Burns Collection. SRA DS 6/15 & 6/16.**

Prior consultation advisable.

**Mon-Tue, Thu-Fri 1000-1300, 1400-1900; Wed 1000-1300; Sat
1000-1300, 1400-1700.**

In the town centre off the High St; bus station in Kingsgate
Shopping Centre; parking at rear.

**Primary source material: Census enumeration books 1841-1881
for Dunfermline [mfilm]; OPR for Dunfermline 1561-1854
[mfilm]; Aberdour Poor Register 1845 [MS]; Fife deaths
1822-1854 [typescript]; Monumental inscriptions (pre-1855) in
West Fife [typescript]; Dunfermline Burgh Voters' Rolls 1832,
1852, 1856, 1868, 1970; Western District of Fife Voters' Rolls**

1846, 1860; West Fife Echo 1900-1932 [mfilm]; Dunfermline Journal 1851-1951 (incomplete) [mfilm]; Dunfermline Press 1859- (incomplete), 1859-1897 [mfilm]; Rosyth & Inverkeithing Journal 1940-1951 [mfilm]; directories, almanacs and registers for Dunfermline, Fife and Kinross 1814-1912 [printed]; collection of Minute Books for various societies, including Niffler Society and the Incorporation of Weavers; Dunfermline Abbey Kirk Session records and Extracts from the Burgh records of Dunfermline in the 16th & 17thC.

Publications: A guide to the Library and Museum Service; Tracing your ancesters: a guide to sources in the Central Library (1981); Local maps: a revised guide. - 1988; The Kingdom of Fife. - 1985. Everyday life in Dunfermline in the late 18th century. - 1978; Dunfermline linen: an outline history. - 1986; Coalmining in West Fife: a bibliography of material held in Dunfermline Central Library; The 17thC witch craze in West Fife: a guide to the printed sources. - 1980; leaflets: George Reid Collection, Murison Burns Collection, Andrew Carnegie.

Photocopies: A3, A4. Milm/mfiche prints: A3, A4.

70   **Dunfermline District Museums**

Viewfield Terrace, DUNFERMLINE KY12 7HY
Tel.: 0363-721814
Contact: The Curator.

Local history collections include papers, photographs and books relating to local industries (linen, coalmining etc.) and social life.

Prior consultation advisable.

Mon-Sat 1100-1700.

Near town centre, Viewfield Terrace is off East Port; 5 mins walk from bus and rail stations; parking adjacent; limited disabled access.

Primary source material: Miscellaneous papers associated with damask linen industry in Dunfermline, including pattern books, printed machine catalogues, MS & printed designs, photographs, guildry books; miscellaneous papers concerned with other local industries & social life in the District including coalmining material.

Publications: Leaflets: Historic Dunfermline; Pittencrieff House Museum.

Photocopies: A3, A4. Photographic copying.

71   E A Hornel, Art Gallery & Library

Broughton House, High Street, KIRKCUDBRIGHT DG6 4JX
Tel.: 0557-30437
Contact: Mr Russell Denwood (Librarian/Curator)

The Hornel Library is a large collection (21000+ items) principally of local history covering Dumfries and Galloway and includes works relating to mainly Scottish art and a fine MS collection of local items. An extensive Burns collection and a general library of books written by locals or relating to the area and includes maps, photos, sasines.

Visitors by appointment.

Mon, Wed-Fri 1100-1300, 1400-1600.

The library is situated within Broughton House, E A Hornel's outstanding residence in Kirkcudbright; bus services and parking near.

Primary source material: Kirkcudbright Parish and Burgh valuation rolls 1850s-1940s; voters lists; ancient valuation rolls; Hornel's letters; C K Sharpe material; McMath-Childe correspondence; Border ballads; Register of Great Seal; calendars 1195-; sasines, etc. 1515-; many scrapbooks (most indexed).

Publications: Computerised subject and newspaper lists; family history lists; Hornel's own cutting book; Kirkcudbright Times 1859 [mfiche].

Photocopies: A3, A4, A5.

72   East Kilbride District Libraries: Central Library

The Olympia, EAST KILBRIDE G74 1PG
Tel.: 03552-20046
Contact: Mr John McLeish

Local history collection includes material relating to East Kilbride & District and the former parishes in the area.

Mon-Tue, Thu-Fri 0945-1945; Wed, Sat 0945-1700.

In the Olympia shopping & leisure centre in the town centre; adjacent to the Central bus station and parking facilities; disabled access.

Primary source material: 1000 books and pamphlets; 500 maps [mainly photocopies]; local newspapers 1856- [945 printed volumes & 100 reels mfilm]; small collection of photographs; OPRs and census returns for East Kilbride District and for some other areas in Lanarkshire and Renfrewshire [mfilm].

Publications: Pamphlet on history of local transport; 15 small pamphlets on aspects of local history, mainly designed for children.

Photocopies: A3, A4.

73   **East Kilbride District Libraries: Strathaven Library**

Glasgow Road, STRATHAVEN ML10 6LZ
Tel.: 0357-21167
Contact: Mrs Connor

Local history collection is a small collection of mainly contemporary material plus photographs and books covering the area.

Mon, Thu-Fri 1400-1945; Tue-Wed, Sat 0945-1300, 1400-1700.

North side of town centre; bus service near; parking; disabled access.

Publications: List available.

Photocopies: A4.

74   **East Lothian Antiquarian and Field Naturalists' Society**

c/o S.A. Bunyan, Inchgarth, East Links, DUNBAR EH42 1LT
Tel.: 0368-63335
Contact: Mr S A Bunyan (Secretary)

A collection of books of local interest deposited with the East Lothian District Local History Centre; and documents deposited with the SRO, list available.

Publications: Transactions East Lothian Antiquarian and Field Naturalists' Society Vols.I-XVIII; Dunbar Parish Church 1342-1987. - 1987; Bibliography of East Lothian. - 1936; Biographies East Lothian - 1941.

75   East Lothian Library Service: Local History Centre

Haddington Branch Library, Newton Port, HADDINGTON EH41
3NA
Tel.: 0620-82 2531   Fax: 0620-82 5735
Contact: Mrs Veronica Wallace
Contact's tel.no.: 0620-82 4161 x326.

**The Local History Centre houses a comprehensive collection of
books on people, places and events in East Lothian, plus
articles, journals, maps, plans, photographs and ephemera.**

Visitors by appointment outwith opening hours.

Mon 1400-1800; Tue 1000-1300, 1400-1900; Thu-Fri 1400-1700.

Newton Port is in the town centre off Market St; bus route near;
free parking opposite.

**Primary source material: Census enumeration books 1841-1891
[mfilm]; valuation rolls 1899-1988 but for Royal Burghs
1930-1988 only [mfiche]; OPRs 1650-1854 (gaps) [mfilm]; IGI to
OPRs for Berwickshire, East Lothian, Midlothian; Register of
sasines: person index 1599-1660, abridgements 1781-1947, and
after 1858 includes synopses of deeds of conveyance; East
Lothian annual registers and yearbooks 1820-1970 (gaps);
Haddingtonshire/East   Lothian   Courier   1859-   [mfilm];
Musselburgh   News   1889-   [part   mfilm];   collection   of
miscellaneous archival and MS records.**

Publications: Local History Centre leaflet, lists of publications and
miscellaneous archival and MS records. Publications range from
Edwardian East Lothian - the journeys of W.F. Jackson 1910-1914,
to reproductions of Golf book of East Lothian / Rev. J. Kerr. -
1896, and Haddington then and now / George Angus. - 1991, and
Gravestones of East Lothian / Islay Donaldson. - 1992; plus
facsimile maps of East Lothian (1736), Dunbar (1830), Haddington
(1819) and Prestonpans (1893).

Photocopies: A3, A4. Mfilm/mfiche prints.

76   Eastwood District Libraries: Local History Collection

Council Offices, Eastwood Park, Rouken Glen Road, GLASGOW
G46 6UG
Tel.: 041-638 1101 x233
Contact: Mrs Maud Devine

Local history collection comprises books, 400 photographs, maps, memorabilia, pamphlets and primary material on Eastwood District with general works on Renfrewshire and Glasgow. There is a small collection of information on the Eaglesham area held at the Eaglesham branch library.

Mon-Thu 0845-1700; Fri 0900-1600.

At Eastwood Toll; bus service; parking.

Primary source material: Unpublished archive material: local authority records 1896-; ratepayers association minutes 1908-; valuation rolls for Mearns 1897-, and Eaglesham 1930-; The Crum Memorial Library accounts; memorabilia, letters, documents donated by local people; map collection includes early County maps, OS, local plans and Ainslie's estate plans of the Eglinton lands; 'Browsing folders' of information on Eastwood, Busby, Clarkston, Giffnock, Thornliebank, Newton Mearns.

Publications: The Eastwoodian (a twice yearly local history bulletin); booklets on the history of Busby, Clarkston, Eaglesham, Giffnock, Mearns, Thornliebank; Eastwood District history & heritage; Greenbank House & Estate.

Photocopies: A3, A4. Local history photographs on request and also on postcards.

77   Edinburgh Architectural Association

15 Rutland Square, EDINBURGH EH1 2BE
Tel.: 031-229 7205
Contact: Mrs A Anderson

A collection of mainly 19thC material covering architecture in Scotland, especially Edinburgh.

Prior consultation advisable. Visitors by appointment.

Mon-Fri 1000-1200.

West end Princes St by Caledonian Hotel; limited metered parking; bus routes near.

78   **Edinburgh City Archives**

Department of Administration, City Chambers, High Street, EDINBURGH EH1 1YJ
Tel.: 031-225 2424 x5196   Fax: 031-220 1494
Contact: Mrs Margaret McBryde (Archivist); Mr Richard Hunter (Archivist)

Houses the official records of the Burgh and City of Edinburgh, formerly Edinburgh Corporation, now City of Edinburgh District Council.

Prior consultation advisable. No charge for historical research. Production fee (minimum £20.00) for requests for Dean of Guild/Building Control plans.

Public Search Room 1/7. Mon-Thu 0930-1600; Fri 0930-1530.

City Chambers opposite St Giles Cathedral on High St; Waverley Railway Station 0.25 miles; St Andrews Square Bus Station and St James Centre car park 0.5 miles; limited street parking; limited disabled access.

Primary source material: Town Council Minutes 1551-1875 [MS], 1875- [printed]; Committee Minutes c1860-1906 [MS], 1907- [printed]; Dean of Guild plans 1762-1975; Building Control plans 1975-; Registers of Burgesses and Guildbrethren, vols.1-26, 1487-1955 [MS]; Registers of Burgesses and Guildbrethren, 2 vols., 1406-1841 [printed]; small number of private deposits.

Publications: Enquirers guide to Building Control plans.

Photocopies: A3, A4. Plans & drawings: A0, A1, A2, A3, A4.

79   **Edinburgh City Libraries: Edinburgh Room**

Central Public Library, George IV Bridge, EDINBURGH EH1 1EG
Tel.: 031-225 5584 x233   Fax: 031-225 8783
Contact: Miss Sheena McDougall

The Edinburgh Room contains an extensive collection of printed information on the people, places, events and history of the City of Edinburgh, including the former burghs of Leith, Portobello and Queensferry. The collection includes books, journals, press cuttings, MS, maps, plans, prints, photographs, slides and ephemera.

Prior consultation advisable.

Mon-Fri 0900-2100; Sat 0900-1300.

City Centre location: Waverley railway station 0.5 miles; St Andrew Square bus station 0.75 miles; buses pass door; parking long stay (Potter Row 0.5 miles); parking meters nearby; parking outside library evenings only; disabled access.

Primary source material: Census enumeration books 1841-1881 [mfilm]; OPRs [mfilm]; valuation rolls 1914- [printed]; voters lists 1856- (incomplete) [printed]; newspapers 1753-, plus isolated earlier issues (several titles); miscellaneous archival and MS records; Edinburgh & Leith post office directories 1773-1974 [printed].

Publications: Edinburgh Room information leaflets. List of publications including postcards, booklets, old OS maps, prints and booklets produced by other organisations available.

Photocopies: A3, A4. Colour photocopies: A3, A4. Mfilm/mfiche prints.

80   Edinburgh City Libraries: Scottish Library

Central Public Library, George IV Bridge, EDINBURGH EH1 1EG
Tel.: 031-225 5584   Fax: 031-225 8783
Contact: Miss M H Burgess

Collection of more than 65000 books and pamphlets on Scottish life, of which 14000 are available on loan. 4000 plus prints and photographs including the Dr I.F. Grant collection of Highland folk life: maps, mfilms, mfiche, cassettes, videos. Government publications, periodicals, news cuttings collection. Particularly strong collection of family histories.

Prior consultation advisable.

Mon-Fri 0900-2100; Sat 0900-1300.

For location see previous entry.

Primary source material: OPRs and Census returns for counties comprising Lothian Region and Borders Region 1841-1881 [mfilm]; valuation rolls for counties comprising Lothian Region 1890-1988 [mfilm]; index to service of heirs [printed]; index to register of deeds [printed]; index to register of sasines [printed]; local directories; newpapers, Glasgow Herald 1885- [mfilm], index 1906-1984 [printed].

Publications: Scottish Library information leaflet.

Photocopies: A3, A4, staff copying of restricted items. Colour photocopies: A3, A4. Mform prints.

81   Edinburgh City Museums: Huntley House & People's Story Museums

142 Canongate, EDINBURGH EH8 8DD
Tel.: 031-225 2424   Fax: 031-557 3346
Contact: Ms Helen Clark; Mr David Scarratt
Contact's tel.no: 031-225 2424 x6687/6682.

The collections of Huntly House and People's Story Museum (163 Canongate) contain material from the 16thC to the present day. This includes photographic and oral tape archives relating to the history of Edinburgh and its people.

Visitors by appointment.

Mon-Sat 1000-1700 (Oct-May), 1000-1800 (June-Sept); Sundays 1200-1700 (Edinburgh Festival).

Canongate is part of the Royal Mile; Waverley railway station 0.5 miles; St Andrews Square Bus Station 0.75 miles; city buses pass door; limited metered parking nearby; limited disabled access.

Primary source material: Records, letters, documents, books, newspapers, brochures, local regulations, acts and proclamations. Subjects include trade records (trade incorporations, companies, firms, trade directories, advertisements, diplomas, indentures); labour records (cards, certificates, trade union cards, rule books, Co-operative Society yearbooks, annuals); Friendly Society and temperance material; theatre programmes & tickets; commemorative material. The photographic archive includes local views and topography, domestic life, housing, personal life, health and welfare, trade unions and politics, leisure, entertainment, warfare, working life. The oral tape archive consists of 200 tapes on aspects of life in Edinburgh in the 20thC. Special collections include archive material relating to Holyrood Glassworks, Norton Park Glassworks, Buchans Thistle Pottery, Field Marshall Earl Haig.

Publications: Huntly House guidebook, 'People's Story' book plus information leaflets.

Photocopies and photographs can be supplied.

82   Edinburgh City Museums: Lady Stair's House

Lady Stair's Close, Lawnmarket, EDINBURGH EH1 2PA
Tel.: 031-225 2424 x6679 Fax: 031-557 3346
Contact: Ms Elaine Finnie

Lady Stair's house contains MS, books, photographs, portraits, sculpture and memorabilia relating to Robert Burns, Sir Walter Scott and Robert Louis Stevenson.

Visitors by appointment.

Mon-Sat 1000-1700 (Oct-May); Mon-Sat 1000-1800 (Jun-Sep); Sun 1200-1700 (Edinburgh Festival).

In Lady Stair's Close off the Lawnmarket (top of Royal Mile); City buses nearby; Waverley railway station 0.3 miles; St Andrews Square Bus Station 0.5 miles; parking nearby.

Primary source material: MS poems, songs, correspondence and family papers. Biographies and various editions of works.

Publications: Lady Stair's House guidebook. Leaflets giving biographical details of Burns, Scott & Stevenson.

Photocopies and photographs can be supplied.

83   Edinburgh City Museums: Lauriston Castle

2A Cramond Road South, EDINBURGH EH4 5QD
Tel.: 031-336 2060
Contact: Mr David Scarratt (Keeper Applied Art Collections)
Contact's tel.no.: 031-225 2424 x6682.

Collection of photographs.

Visitors by appointment.

Laurieston Castle is 4 miles NW of the City Centre at Davidsons Mains; bus service (41) stops at gate, 200 yds to castle; parking; disabled access difficult.

Primary source material: Photographs relating to Morison & Co, cabinetmakers, George St, Edinburgh; interiors of 4 Glenorchy Terrace, Edinburgh (1896); 78 George St, gas lit (1894) and with electricity installed (1896).

Photocopies and photographs can be supplied.

84   **Edinburgh City Museums: Museum of Childhood**

42 High Street, EDINBURGH EH1 1TC
Tel.: 031-225 2424
Contact: The Curators.

Part of the collection including toys, games, costumes, and items relating to health, education and pastimes is of Scottish origin. Reference library.

Prior consultation advisable except to see permanent exhibition.

Mon-Sat 1000-1700 (Oct-May); Mon-Sat 1000-1800 (Jun-Sept); Sun 1400-1700 (Edinburgh Festival).

In Royal Mile; Waverley railway station 0.25 miles; St Andrews Square Bus Station 0.5 miles; city buses pass door; limited metered parking nearby; limited disabled access.

Primary source material: Photographs of children.

Publications: Leaflet available.

Photocopies and photographs can be supplied.

85   **Edinburgh City Museums: South Queensferry Museum**

High Street, South Queensferry, EDINBURGH EH30 9HN
Tel.: 031-331 1590
Contact: Ms Helen Clark
Contact's tel.no.: 031-225 2424 x6687.

Museum contains material relating to the history of the Burgh and its people from the 16thC to the present day.

Prior consultation advisable.

Mon-Sat 1000-1300, 1400-1700 (Summer only).

In the centre of South Queensferry 8 miles west of Edinburgh; on bus route; parking nearby.

Primary source material: Records, letters, documents, books, newspapers, brochures, local regulations, acts and proclamations, and photographs.

Photocopies and photographs can be supplied.

86   Edinburgh University: Main Library

George Square, EDINBURGH EH8 9LJ
Tel.: 031-650 1000   Fax: 031-667 9780
Contact: Mr J V Howard (Special Collections Librarian)
Contact's tel.no.: 031-650 3412.

Collections in the Main Library and the specialist subject collections in the Faculty libraries are rich in books, periodicals, maps and medieval and modern MS of interest for local and especially historical studies. Subject access to the older collections must be via subject bibliographies and the guardbook author catalogue.

Prior consultation advisable, visitors must register as external users. Special collections enquiries: 031-650 8379. Admission free; borrowing on subscription; genealogical search £32.30.

Mon-Thu 0900-2200; Fri 0900-1700; Sat 0900-1230 (term); Mon-Fri 0900-1700 (vacation).

SW corner of George Square; buses near; pay and display car parking nearby; disabled access.

Primary source material: The University Collection includes most of the university's archives to 1920 [MS and printed]. More recent material includes ephemeral memorabilia of student life at the university. This collection and the Medical Archive Centre form a major resource on the history of medicine in Edinburgh in the 18th, 19th and 20thC. The Laing Charters and other Laing Collections include medieval and modern MS sources on local areas and buildings. The Edinburgh Collection of architectural drawings and plans include those by William Playfair, Sir Rowand Anderson and other notable Edinburgh architects. Older collections of printed books include many 19thC published local histories. The map collection includes many historical maps of most areas of Scotland.

Publications: Printed guides and lists of publications available.

Photocopies: A2, A3, A4. Positive mfiche and positive or negative prints are available, subject to the preservation of the original.

87   Edinburgh University: New College Library

Mound Place, EDINBURGH EH1 2LU
Tel.: 031-225 8400
Contact: Mr M C T Simpson (Librarian)

Good collection on local congregations, churches and parishes of Scotland.

Visitors by appointment.

Mon-Fri 0900-1730 (term); Mon-Fri 0900-1700 (vacation).

In city centre; Waverley railway station 0.25 miles; St Andrew Square bus station 0.5 miles; on bus routes; short stay car parking nearby, long stay 0.5 miles; disabled access, enquire in advance.

Primary source material: Varied MS material covering many local congregations, churches and parishes of Scotland.

Photocopies: A4; photographic reproductions via Edinburgh University Main Library.

88   Edinburgh University: School of Scottish Studies

27 George Square, EDINBURGH EH8 9LD
Tel.: 031-650 4160
Contact: Mrs Fran Becket; Dr Alan Bruford

A substantial library of local and general publications on Scottish history and culture, and comparative material from other countries. Card indexes to the contents of numerous relevant publications including the old and new statistical accounts. Binders of transcriptions from tapes and box files of newspaper cuttings, pamphlets, questionnaires etc.

Prior consultation advisable.

Mon-Fri 0900-1700.

West side of George Square, bus routes near; meter parking at door, pay & display near; disabled access difficult.

Primary source material: Sound Archive: 7000+ tapes on music and narrative, social history, custom and belief, material culture, history of settlement. Some early cylinder, wire and direct disc recordings.
Place Name Survey: 1000000 excerpted names; 500 tapes.
Photographic, Film & Video Tape Archive: 10000+ negatives; slide collection, a number of film and video tapes; Tale Archive:

6000+ texts and 2000 index cards; The John Levy Collection: c700 tapes, several thousand slides and photographs, some 16mm cine films, 338 discs of music from different countries; The Will Forret Collection: 2000 commercial discs, several hundred cassette recordings.
MS and typescripts: Dr. R.C. MacLagan's collections on highland folklore; Lady Evelyn Stewart-Murray's collection of gaelic traditional tales; The Linguistic Survey of Scotland (written and recorded data on Gaelic and lowland Scots dialects and varieties of Scottish English).

89   **Fala, Soutra & District History & Heritage Society**

Secretary: Mrs Jean Blades, 5 Fala Village, PATHHEAD EH37 5SY
Tel.: 087-533-248
Contact: Mrs Jean Blades (Secretary)

Photographs and exhibition material (history & World War II); inventory of archives in Midlothian District Library Service.

Visitors by appointment.

Fala Village is 3 miles south of Pathhead on A68 road.

Primary source material: SHARP reports nos. 1,2 & 3 (Soutra medieval hospital excavation reports); extracts from Church records and miscellaneous papers; photographs and transparencies, early 20thC to current archaeological excavations at Soutra medieval hospital.

Publications: Fala & Soutra: past & present / D. & J. Blades. - 1987.

90   **Falkirk District Council. Department of Leisure Services: Falkirk Library**   01324-506800

Hope Street, FALKIRK FK1 5AU
Tel.: 0324-24911 x2316/2259 Fax: 0324-27356
01324-503605

Collection of 15000 items including books, maps, newspapers, pamphlets and ephemera, plus a small collection of photographs and slides covering the Falkirk district.

Prior consultation advisable.

Mon-Tue, Thu 0930-2000; Wed, Fri-Sat 0930-1700.

West of town centre near railway & bus stations.

Primary source material: 5 local newspapers 1845- [mainly on mfilm], some have been indexed; an indexed newspaper clipping collection [printed]; Scottish Metalworkers' Union minutes; Town Council minutes; local Census returns and OPRs [mfilm]; a collection of local publishing; some local films and videos of local events.

Publications: Books, booklets, information sheets, maps and postcards, list available.

Photocopies A3, A4. Mfilm prints: A4.

91   Falkirk Museum

15 Orchard Street, FALKIRK
Tel.: 0324-24911 x2472
Contact: The Curator.

Specialises in social/industrial history. Extensive photographic collection 1855-. Documentary archive of 30000 items 16thC-.

Prior consultation advisable.

Mon-Sat 1000-1230, 1330-1700.

Museum close to town centre, rail & bus stations and parking near.

Primary source material: Boness Seabox Society material, Grangemouth Dockyard ship plans, trial books, large foundry catalogue collection; local photographers collections including Telfer Drummond and Thomas Easton with a total of 19000 photographs subject indexed; information on various local industries including brick making and foundries.

Publications: General information leaflet.

Photocopies: A4. Photographic prints to order.

92   Fife Family History Society

c/o Mr E K Collins, 24 Beveridge Road, KIRKCALDY KY1 1UX
Tel.: 0592-269209
Contact: Mr E K Collins (Membership Secretary)

Very small genealogical library.

Visitors by appointment.

Near to railway station.

Publications: Information sheet available.

93   Fife Folk Museum

The Weigh House, High Street, Ceres, CUPAR KY15 5NF
Tel.: 0334-82380
Contact: A D Mackay (Hon Curator)

Collection of photographs, slides, postcards, books, newspapers, cuttings and ephemera relating to the social, economic & cultural history of bygone Fife.

Prior consultation advisable. Admission: adult £1.00, OAP 0.80p.

Mon, Wed-Sun 1415-1700 (Easter-end Oct).

Near the Cross on the main road; bus services near; parking behind the museum; limited disabled access.

Primary source material: There is a diverse collection of original material including accounts, old advertisements, catalogues, etc. Detailed lists not available but individual requests for information welcomed.

Publications: 6 booklets on Castles of North Fife; Guidebook to the museum; 2 booklets on Central & North Fife.

94   Fife Health Board: Library

Glenrothes House, North Street, GLENROTHES KY7 6HZ
Tel.: 0592-754355 x211   Fax: 0592-756552
Contact: Ms Jill Bennet

Registrar General, local government and public health reports.

Visitors by appointment.

Mon-Thu 0900-1700; Fri 0900-1630.

In town centre, bus terminal nearby; free parking.

Primary source material: Detailed annual report of Registrar General, births, deaths and marriages in Scotland 1861-; annual report of the Local Government for Scotland 1894-1915; annual report of the Board of Supervision for the Relief of the Poor and of Public Health in Scotland 1886-1894; County of Fife

annual reports on the health & sanitary conditions of county and districts 1901-1910.

95   Fife Regional Council: Fife Sites and Monuments Record

Dept. of Economic Development and Planning, Fife House, GLENROTHES KY7 5LT
Tel.: 0592-754411 x6153 Fax: 0592-758582
Contact: Mr Peter Yeoman (Archaeological Officer)

The Fife Sites and Monuments Record is a computer database containing information on 7000+ sites and buildings in Fife, of all periods from the Mesolithic to the present day.

Visitors by appointment.

Mon-Fri 1000-1600.

In centre of Glenrothes; bus routes nearby; free parking; disabled access.

Publications: How to get archaeological advice in Fife; Fife's early archaeological heritage; Excavations at Sinclairtown Pottery, Kirkcaldy.

96   Free Church College: Library

The Mound, EDINBURGH EH1 2LS
Tel.: 031-226 5286 Fax: 031-220 0597
Contact: Professor D Macleod

Scottish ecclesiastical history, including the Highlands and Islands, with Gaelic material.

Prior consultation advisable.

Mon-Fri 0900-1630.

In City Centre; Waverley railway station 0.25 miles; St Andrews Square Bus Station 0.5 miles; on bus routes; street parking nearby; disabled access.

Primary source material: Ecclesiastical documents [printed & MS]; Victorian pamphlets; biographies; archival material relating mainly to Free Church of Scotland; The Witness newspapers.

Photocopies: A3, A4.

97   General Register Office for Scotland

New Register House, Princes St, EDINBURGH EH1 3YY
Tel.: 031-334 0380
Contact: Information desk.

**Main records in the custody of the Registrar General include:
Prior to 1855: OPRs covering births, deaths and marriages
1553-1854; Register of neglected entries 1801-1854. Post 1855:
Registers of births, deaths and marriages; Adopted children
register 1930-; Register of divorces 1984-; Marine register of
births and deaths 1855-; Air register of births and deaths 1948-;
service records 1881-; War register 1899-; registers of births,
deaths and marriages in foreign countries 1860-1965.   Also
Census enumerators' transcript books 1841-1891 [mfilm].**

*Accommodation in the search rooms is limited; seats may be booked
in advance. Fees for searches and extracts are listed in a leaflet.*

Mon-Thu 0900-1630; Fri 0900-1600 (except public holidays).

Access is from West Register St at the east end of Princes St;
Waverley railway station, St Andrews Square Bus Station and
off-street parking nearby.

Publications: General leaflet and list of fees.

98   Glasgow and West of Scotland Family History Society

Mr F Inglis (Hon Secy), 3 Fleming Road, BISHOPTON PA7 5HW
*Contact for publications: Mrs E Galbraith, 11 Deveron Rd,
Bearsden, Glasgow, G61 1LJ.*

Publications: Newsletters; Burial grounds in Glasgow; Strathclyde
sources: a guide for family historians to the genealogical resources
of Argyll & Bute, Ayrshire, Dunbartonshire, Glasgow, Lanarkshire,
Renfrewshire; Census returns & old parochial registers in
microfilm: a directory of public library holdings in the West of
Scotland; Census records for Scottish families. Full list on request.

99   **Glasgow City Libraries: Glasgow Collection**
0141-221-9600

Mitchell Library, North Street, GLASGOW G3 7DN
Tel.: 041-221-7030 x260   Fax: 041-204 4824
Contact: Local Studies Librarian.

The Glasgow Collection comprises over 20000 books along with periodicals, maps, plans, newspapers, illustrations, photographs and ephemera covering a wide range of topics relating to the history of the City, its development and current activities. SRA DS 6/8.

Mon-Fri 0930-2100; Sat 0930-1700.

The Glasgow Collection is in the Mitchell Library New Building, entrance Kent Rd near Charing Cross; parking free but difficult; Charing Cross railway station nearby; Anderson railway station 0.5 miles; bus services for Sauchiehall & St Vincent Sts nearby; disabled access.

Primary source material: Genealogical sources: Voters' rolls 1856-, valuation rolls 1913-89, Census returns 1841-81 [mfilm], cemetery registers, OPRs, Glasgow Post Office directories 1783-1978; over 1000 vols of newspapers from the Glasgow Journal in 1741 to the Glasgow Herald today; early maps from 1773, and OS 1860-; 5000+ illustrations of Glasgow people and places including some original paintings and lithographs; MS including several large collections of family and business papers, North British Locomotive Collection (principally the photographic archive of the North British Locomotive Company and its constituent companies).

Publications: Leaflets: The Mitchell Library, Glasgow Collection: guide; Tracing your ancestors: Mitchell Library and archives sources.

Photocopies: A3, A4. Electrostatic prints: A1, A2, A3, A4. Photographic prints 7x5"-24x20". Mfilm and transparencies.

100   **Glasgow Museums and Art Galleries: Glasgow Art Gallery and Museum**

Kelvingrove, GLASGOW G3 8AG
Tel.: 041-357 3929   Fax: 041-357 4537
Contact: Mrs Meg Buchanan (Depute Keeper Dept of Human History)

Collection of local history items from West of Scotland and Northern Isles.

Visitors by appointment.

Sun 1200-1800; Mon-Wed, Fri-Sat 1000-1700; Thu 1000-2100.

West End of Glasgow near Glasgow University & Western Infirmary; underground station Kelvin Hall (5 min walk); buses pass museum; parking at rear; disabled access at rear basement door.

Primary source material: A small mixed collection of MS and printed documents.

Publications: List available.

Photocopies: A3, A4. Photographic department.

101 Glasgow Museums and Art Galleries: Museum of Transport

Kelvin Hall, 1 Bunhouse Road, GLASGOW G3 8DP
Tel.: 041-357 3929 x304   Fax: 041-357 4537
Contact: Miss Sally Webb (Social History Assistant Keeper)

Large collection of archival material relating to public and private transport in the West of Scotland.

Prior consultation advisable.

Sun 1200-1800; Mon-Sat 1000-1700; Thu 1000-2100 (Summer only).

West End of Glasgow off Old Dumbarton Rd; Kelvin Hall underground station & bus routes near; parking; disabled access by 150 Old Dumbarton Rd.

Primary source material: Plans of Scottish railway locomotives and Glasgow Corporation Transport plans.

Photocopies: A3, A4. Photographic reproductions available.

102 Glasgow Museums and Art Galleries: People's Palace

Glasgow Green, GLASGOW G40 1AT
Tel.: 041-554 0223   Fax: 041-550 0892
Contact: Mrs E Carnegie (Curator); Mr H Dunlop (Curator)

Small collection of photographs, paintings and prints.

Visitors by appointment outwith opening hours.

Sun 1200-1800 (casual visitors only); Mon-Sat 1000-1700.

Located on Glasgow Green; buses going east from Argyle St; parking in museum grounds; disabled access.

Publications: The People's Palace & Glasgow Green; Glasgow stained glass; Scotland sober & free; The strike of the Calton Weavers 1787. List available.

103   Glasgow Museums and Art Galleries: Pollok House

2060 Pollokshaws Road, GLASGOW G43 1AT
Tel.: 041-632 0274
Contact: Mr Brian J R Blench

Estate plans, maps & documentation on Pollok Estate & family history.

Visitors by appointment for access to local history stores & library collection on weekdays.

Sun 1200-1800; Mon-Sat 1000-1700. No access to local history collection at weekends.

3 miles south of City centre & 0.75 mile from Pollokshaws Rd entrance to Pollok Country Park; buses to Pollok Country House entrance, thence internal public transport; parking.

Primary source material: MS covering Pollok Estate and family history.

Photocopies: A4. Photographic service.

104   Glasgow University Archives

GLASGOW G12 8QQ
Tel.: 041-330 5516   Fax: 041-330 4808
Contact: Mr Michael Moss; Mrs Lesley Richmond

The administrative records of Glasgow University date back to the University's foundation in the 15thC, though the bulk of the material dates from the 18thC. There are also collections of records of student and staff societies, the personal papers of students and professors and unrelated collections covering the whole of Scotland.

Visitors by appointment.

Mon-Fri 0900-1700.

In main University buildings, off University Ave, enquire at University Gatehouse. Hillhead underground station 0.25 miles; buses pass on University Ave; car parking nearby; disabled persons access (directions required).

Primary source material: University of Glasgow, Queen Margaret College, Trinity College, Anderson's College of Medicine and Glasgow Veterinary College records; Jackson Collection of Photographs (14000) mainly topographical (1904-1938); Beith parish documents; Hamilton of Rozelle papers; Royal Scottish Academy of Music and Drama records; Glasgow University records relating to administration, finance, students, staff and teaching.

Publications: No published lists - finding aids include computerised catalogues, hand lists & indexes.

Photocopies A3, A4. Photographic reproduction service.

105   Glasgow University Archives: Business Record Centre

13 Thurso Street, GLASGOW G11
Tel.: 041-339 8855 x6079   Fax: 041-330 4808
Contact: Ms Vanna Skelley old 330 -4543

Holds records of businesses throughout Scotland but mainly relating to the West of Scotland; and the former Heriot-Watt University Scottish Brewing Archive.

Visitors by appointment.

Mon-Fri 0900-1230, 1330-1630.

Thurso St (off Dumbarton Rd) opposite Anderson's College/Western Infirmary; Kelvin Hall underground station nearby; buses on Dumbarton Rd; limited on-street car parking.

Primary source material: Shipbuilding records: administrative, financial, technical records & photographs relating to the development of shipbuilding on the Clyde 1830's-late 1970's (John Browns, Alexander Stephens, Simons-Lobnitz, Fleming & Ferguson); House of Fraser archive; administrative, financial and promotional records relating to retail stores; James Finlay plc, textile merchants & manufacturers records; North British Locmotive Co, records, including technical drawings; Andrew Barclay Sons & Co. Ltd., locomotive builders, technical drawings; Anchor Line Ltd, shippers, Glasgow & Edinburgh; J & P Coats Ltd., cotton thread manufacturers, Paisley; Scottish Brewing Archive.

Publications: Summary guide and handlists available.

Photocopies: A3, A4. Photographic reproduction service.

106 Glasgow University Library

Hillhead Street, GLASGOW G12 8QE
Tel.: 041-339 8855 x6754 Fax: 041-357 5043
Contact: Mrs Inez McIntyre

The history section of the Library holds some general secondary material on local history, but is by no means comprehensive, even for the Glasgow area.

Prior consultation advisable.

Mon-Thu 0900-2130; Fri 0900-1700; Sat 0900-1230 (term); Mon-Fri 0900-1700 (Christmas vacation); Mon-Fri 0900-1700; Sat 0900-1230 (Easter and summer vacations).

On Hillhead St (off University Ave, opposite the main University entrance); Hillhead & Kelvinbridge underground stations nearby; bus routes on University Ave; car parking nearby; disabled access and parking via Bute Gardens.

Photocopies: A3, A4. Mform prints: A3, A4. Photographic services.

107 Glasgow University Library: Special Collections Department

Hillhead Street, GLASGOW G12 8QE
Tel.: 041-339 8855 x5630/5631 Fax: 041-357 5043
Contact: Dr Timothy Hobbs (Keeper); Dr Nigel Thorp (Deputy Keeper)

Historical collections relating to Glasgow and the West of Scotland included in Special Collections Department; chiefly printed material, 17th-19thC, but also MS and printed ephemera.

Mon-Thu 0915-2100 (term), 0915-1645 (vacations); Fri 0915-1645; Sat 0915-1215 (except Christmas vacation).

On Hillhead St (off University Ave, opposite the main University entrance); Hillhead and Kelvinbridge underground stations nearby; bus routes on University Ave; car parking nearby; disabled access and parking via Bute Gardens.

Primary source material: Three main collections containing local history material: Euing Collection, library of William Euing (1788-1874), c17500 vols. includes Scottish history, book-sale catalogues, library catalogues; Murray Collection, library of David Murray (1842-1928), c20000 items, a superb regional history collection with a wealth of 17th and 18thC Glasgow imprints, especially Robert Sanders, the Foulis brothers and Robert Urie, 19thC strengths include materials on the economic and social development of the West of Scotland (e.g. works on banking, railways, canals and ports), Scottish newspapers, directories and periodicals, and printed ephemera; Wylie Collection, almost 1000 vols relating to the history and topography of Glasgow and its environs from the 18thC to the early 1900s, includes periodicals and a number of directories, also printed ephemera. Other relevant collections include Socialist pamphlets, 1930s-1950s (Broady and Bissett Collections); military and Scottish music and concerts and variety theatre in Glasow (Farmer Collection); correspondence of William Thomson, Lord Kelvin (Kelvin Papers); correspondence of Alexander MacCallum Scott, Liberal MP for Bridgeton; materials relating to Scottish theatre history, including archives of the Citizens' Theatre and Scottish Ballet (Scottish Theatre Archive).

Publications: A guide to the major collections in the Department of Special Collections. - 1989. (Limited subject access by means of internal typewritten finding aids).

Photocopies: A3, A4. Mform prints: A3, A4. Photographic services.

108   The Gordon Highlanders: Regimental Collection

Viewfield Road, ABERDEEN AB1 7XH
Tel.: 0224-318174
Contact: Major (Retd) D H White (Regimental Secretary)

Depicts life of the regiment.

Visitors by appointment.

1.5 miles west of city centre, off Queens Rd; on bus routes from centre; car parking; disabled access.

Primary source material: Collection includes archives, reference books, and documentation covering the history of the regiment.

109   **Grampian Health Board Archives**

PO Box 119, 1-7 Albyn Place, ABERDEEN AB9 8QP
Tel.: 0224-589901 x75288   Fax: 0224-582947
Contact: Miss F R Watson (Archivist)

The Health Board's archives contain the records of most of the hospitals and health authorities which once existed or still exist in the Grampian area. These date mainly from the mid/late 19thC although some record series date from the 1740s. The archivist also has information on hospital/health records belonging to Highland Health Board.

Visitors by appointment.

Mon-Fri 0900-1700.

Grampian Health Board Headquarters are at the west end of Union St; buses to main entrance and/or within 100 yards; railway station 0.75 miles; restricted car parking nearby; disabled access difficult, contact for details.

Primary source material: Minutes, financial records, patient and staff registers, case notes, nurse training records, annual reports, plans and photographs from over 50 hospitals and nursing homes in the North East; administrative records of bodies set up under various National Health Service (Scotland) Acts (the North-Eastern Regional Hospital Board, Grampian Health Board and their respective constituent boards/units); records of insurance committees, executive councils and local medical committees; some material from local authority health departments including annual reports of medical officers of health, registers of notification of infectious diseases and tuberculosis.

Publications: Copy lists are available in the searchrooms at the SRO. Material is mostly MS or typewritten.

Photocopies: A3, A4. Photographic prints.

110   **Grampian Regional Archives**

Old Aberdeen House, Dunbar Street, ABERDEEN AB2 1UE
Tel.: 0224-481775
Contact: Mrs B Cluer (Regional Archivist)

Archives relate to counties of Aberdeen, Banff, Kincardine & Moray, also City of Aberdeen (education & valuation only) & Burghs now in Banff/Buchan & Gordon Districts and includes schools throughout region.

Visitors by appointment.

Mon-Fri 1000-1300, 1400-1600.

Near King's College, Old Aberdeen; car parking nearby; near bus routes from city centre & railway station; disabled access.

Primary source material: Includes records of parochial boards/parish councils 1845-1930; Commissioners of supply & County councils 17thC -1975; town councils mainly 19thC-1975; schools 19thC -1975; valuation & electoral rolls, varying runs and dates for Counties and Burghs in Grampian Region & includes Aberdeen City and County, Banff & Kincardine Counties; valuation rolls only for Elgin County & Burgh, Moray County, Burghs of Forres and Inverurie; Burgh Council Minutes for Aberchirder, Banff, Ellon, Fraserburgh, Huntly, Inverurie, Kintore, Macduff, Old Meldrum, Peterhead, Portsoy, Rosehearty, Turriff.

Publications: General leaflet available (gives dates for runs).

Photocopies: A3, A4. Photographic reproduction available.

111   Grampian Transport Museum

ALFORD AB33 8AD
Tel.: 09755 62292
Contact: Mr Mike Ward

Collection covers transport development in the North East of Scotland.

Visitors by appointment.

Sun-Sat 1030-1700 (Apr-Sep).

Off main street in Alford, 25 miles west of Aberdeen; parking.

Primary source material: Photographs, slides, vehicle manuals, magazines (including a complete set of Railway Magazine); there are indexes for periodicals, technical literature, general and specific subjects.

Photographs can be supplied.

112   **Greater Glasgow Health Board Archive**

Archives, Glasgow University, GLASGOW G12 8QQ
Tel.: 041-330 5516   Fax: 041-330 4808
Contact: Mr Alistair G Tough (Archivist)

Visitors by appointment; donations welcome.

Mon-Fri 0900-1200; 1400-1700.

In main University building, off University Ave (enquire at gatehouse); Hillhead underground station 0.25 miles; buses pass on University Ave; parking nearby; disabled access, directions required.

Primary source material: Administrative, financial and clinical records of Glasgow hospitals, dispensaries & clinics from 1787; administrative & financial records of Western Regional Hospital Board and constituent Boards of Management 1948-1974, and of Greater Glasgow Health Board 1974-; papers of various organisations and individuals connected with health care in Scotland.

Publications: The archives and guide to the records of the Greater Glasgow Health Board, in Health care as social history: the Glasgow case / O. Checkland and M. Lamb. - 1982.

113   **Gullane Local History Society & Dirleton Local History Group**

c/o Gullane Libary, East Links Road, GULLANE EH31 2AF
Tel.: 0620-842073
Contact: Respective Secretaries, via the Librarian.

Collection comprises photographs, slides, postcards and miscellaneous papers depicting life in the two East Lothian villages.

Visitors by appointment.

Mon 1400-1700; Tue 1000-1300; Thu 1400-2000.

off Main Steet in centre of village; parking; bus route nearby.

Primary source material: Miscellaneous papers; 150 photographs (mostly 1910-1914 Gullane); 200 slides mostly early 20thC; postcards etc. depicting life in the villages (all indexed); exhibition material covering World War II in Gullane.

Publications: Booklets: Reminiscences no.1; Gullane Parish Church 1888-1988; Dirleton collected essays 1985 & 1989.

114   Hamilton District Libraries: Local Studies Department

98 Cadzow Street, HAMILTON ML3 6HQ
Tel.: 0698-282323 x143
Contact: Mrs Isabel Walker (Reference Librarian)

The Local History Collection comprises c6500 items (books, maps, photographs, newspapers etc.) covering Lanarkshire in general and Hamilton District in particular. SRA DS 6/4.

Prior consultation advisable.

Mon-Tue, Thu-Fri 1000-1900; Wed 1000-1300; Sat 1000-1700.

Central location, 5 mins walk from town centre and 10 mins from bus & railway stations; limited street parking; disabled access difficult, prior contact advised.

Primary source material: Census returns 1841-1881 and OPRs [mfilm]; newspapers: Hamilton Advertiser 1856- and Hamilton Herald continued as Lanarkshire 1888-1915 [mfilm]; maps of Hamilton area 1781- and OS maps 1860-; Hamilton Town Council Minutes 1701-1975 and Abstract of Accounts 1879-1975; Hamilton Police Commissioners Minutes 1857-1901; Hamilton Water Works Commissioners Minutes 1854-1901; Hamilton Combination Poor House (later Hamilton Home) Minutes 1864-1975; Hamilton Burgh Register of Electors 1851-1975 (early years incomplete); directories of Hamilton, 1847-1909 (various years); Lanark County Council Minutes 1890-1975 (incomplete).

Publications: Leaflets; A guide to the Local History Collection and services; source lists for individual localities; leaflets describing holdings of newspapers, census returns, OS maps etc; publications for sale.

Photocopies: A3, A4. Mfilm/mfiche prints. Limited photographic prints service.

115   Hamilton District Museum

129 Muir Street, HAMILTON ML3 6BJ
Tel.: 0698-283981   Fax: 0698-458663
Contact: The Curator.

Small collection of maps and photographic material.

Mon-Tue 1000-1700; Wed-Sat 1000-1200, 1300-1700.

Near town centre and bus routes; parking nearby, limited disabled access, prior contact advised.

Primary source material: Maps c1790-1860 [MS & printed]; archival documents (e.g. colliery letter books) [MS]; photographs c1860-; glass negatives, glass positives, prints, dageurrotypes.

Photocopies: A3, A4. Photographs 10x8" b&w prints.

116 Hawick Archaeological Society: Historical Collection

Public Library, North Bridge Street, HAWICK TD9 9QT
Tel.: 0450-72637
Contact: Mr H Mackay (Reference Librarian); Mr Ian Landles
(Secretary of the Society)
Contact's tel.no.: 0450-75546 (Secretary).

Local History Collection comprises books and material covering Hawick and District. NB Some earlier material and books were donated to the Hawick Museum (qv). A more comprehensive collection of material for Hawick and district is kept in the Borders Region Local History and Archive Centre at Selkirk (qv).

Prior consultation advisable.

Mon, Wed-Fri 0900-1900; Tue 0900-1730.

Library located in town centre; on bus route; parking at rear.

Primary source material: Incorporated trades MS.

Publications: Annual transactions of the Society.

117 Heriot-Watt University: Archive

Riccarton Campus, Riccarton, EDINBURGH EH14 4AS
Tel.: 031-449 5111 x4064 Fax: 031-449 5153
Contact: Dr Norman H Reid (The Archivist)

The University Archive holds collections relating to the university and its predecessor institutions, the Riccarton Estate, the Currie & Balerno area, and other educational institutions, etc., in the Edinburgh area.

Visitors by appointment.

Mon-Fri 0930-1630.

The University Archive is located in the Library/Language Building on the Riccarton Campus, signposted off the Calder Rd (A71) & the Lanark Rd (A70), 8 miles west of Edinburgh city centre; bus service direct to campus; parking; disabled access.

Primary source material: Official records of the Edinburgh School of Arts 1821-1854, the Watt Institution and School of Arts 1854-1885, Heriot-Watt College 1885-1966, and Heriot-Watt University 1966-, committee papers, academic records, correspondence, photographs, films, press cuttings, etc.; family papers of the Gibson-Craig Family, proprietors of Riccarton, including estate papers (titles, etc.) 15th-19thC, rentals, accounts, etc., & 19thC correspondence; The Tweedie Collection of material (books, papers, photocopies, photographs & artefacts) relating to the history of the Currie & Balerno area; records (official & photographic) of Leith Nautical College 1855-1987; also small reference collection of books, pamphlets, etc. on Edinburgh educational history and of material relating to James Watt.

Publications: Guides to archival holdings (incomplete) and occasional leaflets on the history of the University.

Photocopies: A3, A4.

118   Highland Health Board: Archives

c/o Highland Health Sciences Library, Raigmore Hospital, INVERNESS IV2 3UJ
Tel.: 0463-234151 x313   Fax: 0463-713454
Contact: Mrs Higgins (Librarian)

The Health Board's archives contain the records of many of the hospitals and health authorities which once existed or still exist in the Highland area. These date mainly from the mid/late 19thC although some of the records of the (Royal) Northern Infirmary date from c1800.

Visitors by appointment.

Mon-Fri 0900-1700.

Situated within Highland College of Nursing/Postgraduate Medical Centre on the Raigmore Hospital site, 1.5 miles east of town centre; railway station 1.5 miles; bus services to hospital's main entrance 400 yards from library; parking; disabled access.

Primary source material: Minutes, financial records, patient and staff registers, case notes, nurse training records, annual records & some plans and photographs from most of the hospitals in the north of Scotland; administrative records of the Northern Regional Hospital Board and its constituent boards of management set up under N.H.S.(Scotland) Act 1947; also some material from local authority health departments including annual reports of the Medical Officers of Health and Registers of Notification of Infectious Disease.

Photocopies: A3, A4. Photographic prints can be supplied.

119   Highland Regional Library Service and Regional Archives

Inverness Public Library, Farraline Park, INVERNESS IV1 1NH
Tel.: 0463-236463 Fax: 0463-237001
Contact: Mr P D Reynolds; Mr R D Steward (Regional Archivist); Miss C Goodfellow (Branch Librarian)
Contacts' tel.nos.: 0463-235713 (Mr Reynolds); 0463-220330 (Regional Archivist).

Main collection in Inverness consists of 30000+ items, including the library of the Inverness Gaelic Society, Fraser-Mackintosh Collection and the Inverness Kirk Session Library (founded c1705). There are small local collections in the libraries at Brora, Dingwall, Fort William, Nairn, Thurso and Wick. SRA DS 6/5.

Prior consultation advisable, sliding scale of charges for genealogical searches (Library); visitors by appointment (Archives).

Mon, Fri 0900-1930; Tue, Thu 0900-1830; Wed, Sat 0900-1700 (Library); Mon-Fri 0900-1700 (Archives).

Farraline Park is in the town centre, off Academy St; bus station at the library; railway station and parking nearby; disabled access.

Primary source material: Library: Local newspapers [printed & mfilm]; genealogical materials including OPRs and census returns [mfilm].
Archives: Minutes and other official archives of the former counties of Inverness-shire, Ross & Cromarty, Sutherland and Caithness from early 18thC-1975 (including valuation rolls from 1870s, parochial and school board records, school log books); Inverness Burgh archives 1556-1975 (including valuation rolls, registers of sasines, court records, trades guild records); Inverness-shire Sheriff Court records 1700-1900; Highland farm and estate records, especially Skye, Knoydart and Newhall 1780-1940; records of various businesses, societies, institutions 18th-20thC.

Publications: Local history and Ancestors leaflets.

Photocopies: A3, A4. Mfilm/mfiche prints: A3, A4.

120   Institute of Bankers in Scotland

19/20 Rutland Square, EDINBURGH EH1 2DE
Tel.: 031-229 9869 Fax: 031-229 1852
Contact: Dr C W Munn (Secretary)

Library includes a special collection covering banking histories.

Prior consultation advisable.

Mon-Fri 0900-1300, 1400-1700.

West end of Princes St by Caledonian Hotel; limited metered parking; bus routes near.

Primary source material: Banking documents and Scottish bank notes.

Photocopies: A4.

121   Inverclyde District Libraries: Watt Library

9 Union Street, GREENOCK PA16 8JH
Tel.: 0475-20186 01475 - 720181
Contact: Mrs Couperwhite (Local History Assistant)

Comprehensive range of local material including photographs, newspapers, genealogical, burgh records, and material on businesses and eminent people. SRA DS 6/6.

Prior consultation advisable.

Mon, Thu 1400-1700, 1800-2000; Tue, Fri 1000-1300, 1400-1700; Wed, Sat 1000-1300.

Close to town centre; bus terminals and Greenock West railway station near; parking nearby.

Primary source material: OPRs and census records for Renfrewshire [mfilm]; trade directories; burgh material; cemetery records; shipbuilding & Clyde Port Authority material (including an index of ship launches on the Lower Clyde); photographs; four local newspapers from 1802; a births, marriages & deaths index covering 1802-1914; local

businesses/companies; information on eminent local figures (James Watt, John Gault & George Blake).

Photocopies: A3, A4. Mfilm copies.

122   Inverness Museum & Art Gallery

Castle Wynd, INVERNESS IV2 3ED
Tel.: 0463-237114   Fax: 0463-233813
Contact: Ms Janet Watson (Assistant Curator (Social History)); Mr Robin Hanley (Assistant Curator (Archaeology) [for maps])

The museum has a small library of books and pamphlets relating to Inverness and district plus photographs, maps and bound volumes of local newspapers.

Visitors by appointment.

Mon-Fri 1000-1700.

In town centre on bus route; parking nearby; disabled access to ground floor.

Primary source material: c300 maps, 18thC-, relating to Inverness and E Ross-shire, Inverness town plans, estate maps, thematic maps showing communications and services, OS maps [MS and printed]; large collection of photographs of Inverness and the Highlands in print and glass negative form; part runs of the Inverness Courier 1915-1983 and the Northern Chronicle 1915-1948; Inverness Town Council minutes 1894-.

Publications: Leaflet about museum, displays and location.

Photocopies: A4.

123   Isle of Arran Heritage Museum

Brodick, ARRAN KA27 8DP
Tel.: 0770-2636
Contact: Mrs I Gorman (Archivist); Mrs V Small (Chairman)
Contacts' tel.nos.: 0770-2693 (Archivist), 0770-2602 (Chairman).

A large collection of material relating to life on Arran includes papers, letters, journals and photographs; a tape collection covering islanders describing life in their youth, plus music and poetry.

Prior consultation advisable.

Mon-Sat 1000-1700 (Easter-Oct); Wed 1030-1530 (Nov-Easter).

1 mile north of Brodick pier; on bus route; parking; disabled access.

Primary source material: A substantial photographic collection features all aspects of life on the island (farming, fishing, housing and family groups) 1870-; papers, journals and correspondence covering genealogy, land tenure, clearances & emigration, geology, archaeology, island life; oral history, music & poetry tapes by islanders.

124   Jordanhill College of Education: Library

76 Southbrae Drive, GLASGOW G13 1PP
Tel.: 041-950 3000   Fax: 041-950 3268
Contact: Mrs M Harrison (Principal Librarian)
Contact's tel.no.: 041-950 3308.

The College Archive contains minute books, photographs, plans, books, periodical articles and other documents dating back to 1828, and relating to the various institutions which are antecedents of Jordanhill College. 19thC reports of the Committee of Council on Education, and the Scottish Education Department are also held. The collection is of interest to those studying the history of education during this period and to enquirers pursuing genealogical research.

Prior consultation advisable.

Mon-Thu 0900-2100; Fri 0900-1700; Sat 0900-1200 (term); Mon-Fri 0900-1700 (vacation).

The library is in the Sir Henry Wood Building; Jordanhill railway station 0.25 miles, Scotstounhill 0.3 miles; parking; disabled access.

Primary source material: Glasgow Infant School visitors book; Glasgow Church of Scotland Training College Committee visiting book 1849-53, Minute book of Committee of Management 1875-77, visitors' book 1851-53, students registers 1857-60, 1864-66 & 1873-91, library catalogue c1880; Glasgow Free Church Training College minute books 1845-60, 1860-91 & 1892-1907, students registers 1845-81, 1849/50-1855/56 & 1855/56-1872/73; class lists and marks 1879-97/98 [MS & mfiche]; Glasgow United Free Church Training College students records 1902-05 [ledgers]; Glasgow University King's Students committee minute book [MS]; Glasgow Provinicial Committee for the Training of Teachers, minutes 1907-59 [printed],

students records 1905-45 [MS]; Jordanhill College Governing Body minutes 1959- [printed]; Hamilton College of Education Governing Body minutes 1966-81 [typescript]; student magazines, certificates, photographs and other memorabilia.

Publications: Typescript catalogue available in library.

Photocopies: A3, A4. Mfilm and mfiche prints: A4. Photographic services available.

125   Kilmarnock and Loudoun District Libraries

Dick Institute, Elmbank Avenue, KILMARNOCK KA1 3BU
Tel.: 0563-26401 x128   Fax: 0563-29661
Contact: Mrs Anne Geddes

Ayrshire Collection includes extensive collections of books, newspapers, magazines, pamphlets on Ayrshire; some books, pamphlets and newspapers have been indexed.

Prior consultation advisable.

Mon-Tue, Thu-Fri 0900-2000; Wed, Sat 0900-1700.

Dick Institute is close to town centre off London Rd; bus station 0.25 miles; railway station 0.5 miles; car parking; disabled person access at rear.

Primary source material: IGI(S,I) 1988 [mfiche]; OPRs for most of Ayrshire [mfiche]; Census returns 1841-1881 for all of Ayrshire [mfiche]; local newspapers 1844- [mfiche]; Kilmarnock directories 1833-1957; Kilmarnock Midwife's register 1777-1829; Kilmarnock Mortality Register 1728-1763; gravestone inscriptions, mostly pre-1855; indexes to intimations in early local newspapers.

Publications: Tracing your family tree; local publications (including pictorial histories of Darvel, Dundonald, Galston & Kilmarnock, and local history of Kilmarnock); pre-1855 gravestone inscriptions.

Photocopies: A3, A4. Mfilm prints: A4.

126 Kincardine Local History Group

c/o Mr Charles O'Donnell, Secretary, 60 Regent Street, Kincardine-on-Forth, ALLOA FK10 4NN
Tel.: 0259-31022
Contact: Mr Bill Wolsey
Contact's tel.no.: 0259-30430.

A general local history of Kincardine & Tulliallan.

Visitors by appointment.

By arrangement.

The Group meets every two weeks from Oct to Mar at the Community Centre, Anderson Lane, Kincardine; specialist collections at Shore House, Forth St, Kincardine-on-Forth.

Primary source material: Notes on the history of Kincardine & Tulliallan [MS]; collection of 1500 photographs & 2000 slides indexed historically & geographically; collection of historical maps of the area.

Publications: Robert Peters, the Tulliallan sailor-poet; Thomas Buchanan, Minister of Tulliallan 1692-1710; A triad of churches; Tulliallan four lads o' pairts: Sir James Wylie, Sir James Dewar, Robert Maule J.P., Sir Robert Maule.

Photocopying and photographic services available by arrangement.

127 Kirkcaldy District Libraries: Reference & Local Studies Department

Central Library, War Memorial Gardens, KIRKCALDY KY1 1YG
Tel.: 0592-260707 ~~(268386)~~ *(01592) 412878*
Contact: Mrs J Klak

The local studies collection covers Fife in general and Kirkcaldy District in detail. Sources include books, maps, photographs, press cuttings, valuation rolls, IGI(S). SRA DS 6/18.

Prior consultation advisable.

Mon-Thu 1000-1900; Fri-Sat 1000-1700.

In town centre adjacent to the railway station; 5 mins walk to the bus station; limited parking; disabled access.

Primary source material: Census returns 1841-81 and OPRs for all Fife parishes [mfilm]; Fife Free Press 1871- [1871-1986 mfilm]; Fifeshire Advertiser 1845-1965 [mfilm]; Leven Advertiser & Wemyss Gazette 1906-39 [mfilm]; Leven Advertiser, Buckhaven & Methil News 1897-1905 [mfilm].

Publications: Local collection and Adam Smith Bicentenary leaflets; Your Scottish roots / S. Campbell & E. Dickson.

Photocopies: A3, A4. Mfilm/mfiche prints: A3, A4. Prints available from photograph collection.

128   **Kirkcaldy Museum & Art Gallery**

War Memorial Gardens, KIRKCALDY KY1 1YG
Tel.: 0592-260732   Fax: 0592-268951
Contact: Ms Dallas Mechan (Curator); Mr Gavin Grant (Assistant Curator)

Original MS and printed material, photographs relating to the social and industrial history of Kirkcaldy District; printed ephemera; files containing information and secondary material on subjects of local interest. SRA DS 6/22.

Prior consultation advisable.

Mon-Sat 1100-1700; Sun 1400-1700 (Curatorial staff available Mon-Fri only).

In town centre adjacent to the railway station; 5 mins walk to bus station; parking; disabled access via adjoining library.

Primary source material: MS estate papers & ledgers relating to Rothes Family (17th-18thC lands & mineworkings); miscellaneous records (incomplete) of local industries (e.g. Burntisland shipyard, Nairns linoleum manufacturers); burgess tickets relating to Burntisland; miscellaneous archive and MS records; maps of Kirkcaldy District; original photographs 1870s-; lantern slides & glass negatives (large group 1930s East Wemyss).

Publications: Leaflets on local history topics; photographic booklet on Burntisland.

Photocopies: A3, A4. Photographic service.

129   Kyle and Carrick District Library Service: Local Collection

Carnegie Library, 12 Main Street, AYR KA8 8ED
Tel.: 0292-269141 x5227
Contact: The Local Studies and Reference Librarians.
Contacts' tel.no.: 0292-286385 (after 1645).

Local collection houses a large collection of books, articles, journals, maps, plans, photographs, newspapers & ephemera relating specifically to Kyle & Carrick District but with coverage for Ayrshire & SW Scotland; includes Burns collection (editions of Burns poetry, criticisms, ephemera), Galt collection (editions of the works of John Galt), and publications of the Ayrshire Archaeological and Natural History Society. SRA DS 6/14.

Prior consultation advisable. Advance booking for mfilm reader necessary, contact Local Studies Librarian or Reference Librarian.

Mon-Tue, Thu-Fri 0900-1930; Wed, Sat 0900-1700.

Local collection is housed in Reference Dept.; Carnegie Library is on Main St near the New Bridge; bus station 0.25 miles; railway station 1 mile; parking nearby; disabled access to ground floor, but no access to local collection.

Primary source material: Census enumeration books 1841-81 [mfilm]; OPRs 1650-1854 [mfilm]; records & charters of the Burgh of Ayr c13thC-1974 [MS & printed]; valuation rolls County of Ayr 1899-1942, Burgh of Ayr 1906-1974, Kyle & Carrick District 1975-; voters rolls Burgh of Ayr 1905-75, Kyle & Carrick District 1975-; newspapers Ayr Advertiser 1803-, Ayrshire Post 1882- (indexed 1900-60), Ayr Observer 1832-1930 [printed plus some mfilm]; calendars of confirmation (Scotland) 1876-1936, 1948-1959; index for Ayrshire sasines 1599-1609, 1617-1660; Ayr directories 1829-1956 (some gaps) plus some Ayrshire directories; Ayr Poor Relief minute book 1872-94 [MS]; Ayr Poor House stent book 1757-1845 [MS].

Publications: Leaflets, Ayrshire Census returns 1841-1881 and OPRs for Ayrshire.

Photocopies: A3, A4. Mfilm/mfiche prints.

130   Lesmahagow Parish Historical Association: Archive

c/o The Archivist, 8 The Crescent, LESMAHAGOW ML11 0DP
Tel.: 0555-893859
Contact: Mr Robert S McLeish (Archivist)

The archive holds a comprehensive collection of articles, journals, maps, plans and photographs covering Lesmahagow Parish, and genealogical files of local families.

Visitors by appointment.

The Archive is held in Lesmahagow High School 0.25 miles from Lesmahagow village; on bus route; parking; disabled access.

Primary source material: OPRs, births/baptisms 1692-1854; proclamations of marriage 1692-1854; register of burials 1765-1844 [mfilm]; 1821 & 1841 census [photocopy] census enumeration books 1851-81 [mfilm]; Linning's list of 1783 [photocopy]; Annals of Lesmahagow / J.B. Greenshields - 1864 (including Poll Tax record of 1695); trade directories 1825-1970 [photocopy]; list of electors 1835 [photocopy]; monumental inscription list for Lesmahagow Churchyard, surveyed 1987; miscellaneous archival records. Transcriptions of OPRs currently being prepared.

Publications: Lesmahagow Parish journals (1986-87) On Two Fronts; Town Crier news letters (1982-90); Lesmahagow: the Parish and the people / W. Clelland - 1990.

Photocopies: A3, A4 by arrangement.

131   Liddesdale Heritage Association

c/o Miss E. Anderson (Secretary), 5 Mid Liddle Street, NEWCASTLETON TD9 0RL
Tel.: 03873-75391
Contact: Miss E Anderson (Secretary); Mr Alexander Armstrong (Chairman)
Contact's tel.no.: 03873-75248 (Chairman).

Miscellaneous collection of local artefacts, photographs and printed historical data.

Visitors by appointment, Oct-Easter.

Mon-Fri 1330-1630; Sat-Sun 1000-1200, 1330-1630 (Easter-Sep).

The Heritage Centre is in the centre of the village at Janet Armstrong House, Douglas Square; limited bus service; parking; disabled access.

Primary source material: Local graveyards records (in progress).

Publications: Leaflets, Castleton and Saughtree Churches; The hill folk; newsletters.

132   Lothian & Borders Fire Brigade: Museum of Fire

Brigade Headquarters, Lauriston Place, EDINBURGH EH3 9DE
Tel.: 031-228 2401 x284   Fax: 031-228 6222
Contact: Fire Officer, Community Education Dept.

The museum tells the story of the formation in 1824 of the oldest municipal fire brigade in the United Kingdom. There is an historical archive and collection of photographs and glass slides.

Visitors by appointment. Donations to Museum Fund accepted.

Mon-Fri 0900-1300 & 1400-1630.

Fire Brigade HQ at the junction of Lady Lawson St & Lauriston Place between Tollcross & Royal Infirmary; on bus routes; parking nearby; disabled access.

Primary source material: Historic records on fire fighting and the fire brigade.

Photocopies by arrangement.

133   Lothian Health Board: Medical Archive Centre

Edinburgh University Library, George Square, EDINBURGH EH8 9LJ
Tel.: 031-650 3392   Fax: 031-667 9780
Contact: Dr Mike Barfoot

Records of hospitals and related institutions in Lothian Region and former counties 1728-. Collection of historical photographs.

Visitors by appointment. Charges for some categories of postal enquiries.

Mon-Fri 0900-1700.

Edinburgh University main library is in George Square; Waverley railway station 1 mile; bus routes near; parking near; disabled access.

Primary source material: Royal Infirmary minutes 1728-; Royal Edinburgh Hospital records early 19thC-; records of many of the hospitals in the region (including those recently closed ie Bruntsfield and Elsie Inglis in Edinburgh); papers relating to notable individuals such as Derek Dunlop and Elsie Stephenson; gifted records of the Medico Chirurgical Society 1821-1971; records of the Edinburgh Blood Transfusion Service; collection of clinical cases.

Publications: Leaflet: Medical Archive Centre.

Photocopies: A3, A4.

134 Lothian Regional Council: Department of Architectural Services

Information Unit, 154 McDonald Road, EDINBURGH EH6 4LA
Tel.: 031-556 9242 x242 Fax: 031-556 8013
Contact: Ms Elizabeth Strachan (Librarian)

Drawings of Lothian Regional Council owned buildings; collection of local history monographs.

Prior consultation advisable.

Mon-Fri 0900-1630.

In former secondary school at junction with Broughton Rd; Waverley railway station & St Andrews Square Bus Station 1 mile; bus routes near; parking; disabled access difficult, check in advance.

Primary source material: Drawings of Lothian Regional Council owned buildings both original and mfilmed.

Full reproduction services available (charge may be levied).

135   The Lynedale Archive

c/o Mrs. I. Paterson, West Linton Historical Association (Trustee),
Dovewood, WEST LINTON EH46 7DS
Tel.: 0968-60346
Contact: Mrs I Paterson (Chairman)

Photographic documentary & printed material covering the Lynedale area of Tweeddale, including the parishes of West Linton, Carlops, Newlands, Kirkurd, Dolphinton.

Visitors by appointment.

The archive is housed in The Village Centre, Raemartin Square, West Linton; bus route nearby; parking; disabled access.

Primary source material: Catalogued collection of 600+ photographs, 800+ slides featuring Lynedale area (social life, transport, trades etc.); project files of source material on local railway, gas works, shops & houses, local trades; comprehensive collection of secondary source material e.g. newspaper excerpts, booklets, articles etc.; collection of maps of area.

Photocopies by arrangement.

136   Macaulay Land Use Research Institute: Library

Craigiebuckler, ABERDEEN AB9 2QJ
Tel.: 0224-318611   Fax: 0224-311556
Contact: Secretary (x204) and Librarian (x212).

Comprises books on historical agriculture and land use pre-1900.

Visitors by appointment only.

Mon-Fri 0845-1245, 1345-1715.

Institute is in the West End of Aberdeen; on bus route; parking.

Primary source material: Geological and land use maps and surveys (current material available for purchase).

Publications: Bibliography no.1 (for books in library); Publications and services (includes climate, soil, land capability maps).

137 Midlothian District Libraries: Local Studies Department

Midlothian District Libraries Headquarters, 7 ~~Station Road,~~ ~~ROSLIN EH25 9PF~~ 2, CLERK ST. LOANHEAD, MIDLOTHIAN
Tel.: 031-440 2210 x226 EH20 · 9DB
(0131-270-7500-PBHe) *Contact: Ms Marion M T Richardson* (Same tel. no. + ext.)

The Local Studies Department has a substantial collection of books covering the present District and former County, including books by and about local people. There is a growing collection of 19thC directories, maps, estate plans, photographs, prints, newspapers, pamphlets, ephemera and printed records; local authorities, local organisations and private archives.

Prior consultation advisable.

Mon 0900-1700, 1800-2000 (not staffed 0900-1245); Tue-Thu 0900-1700; Fri 0900-1545.

Station Rd is off Main St; bus services nearby; parking; disabled access.

Primary source material: lst, 2nd & 3rd sets of Statistical Accounts; reports of RCAHMs; census enumeration books 1841-81 [mfilm]; valuation rolls 1881-1985; OPRs for Midlothian District plus Heriot & Stow to 1854 [mfilm]. IGI 1988 [mfiche]; monumental inscriptions for some Midlothian & East Lothian churchyards; newspapers: Dalkeith Advertiser 1869- [mfilm], South Midlothian Advertiser 1932-52 & 1960-73; photographic collection includes buildings, places and events; map collection: 6" & 25" OS 1855 & 1890s plus OS namebooks [mfilm]; estate plans (include mostly Newton and Penicuik parishes); local authority archives: records of the former Burghs of Bonnyrigg & Lasswade, Dalkeith, Loanhead and Penicuik and former District Councils, some material relating to courts, local bequests, welfare & public health, school boards & Education Committee records 1870-1919, school log books for most Midlothian schools 1870s-mid 20thC; private archives including family papers of the Lucas Family of Dalkeith; Midlothian directories (with gaps) cover the 19thC; index to sasines 1599-1660; register of deeds 1661-1695; index to service of heirs 1700-186; national printed records; registers of Privy Council 1569-1691, Privy Seal 1542-80, Great Seal 1424-1668; documents relating to Scotland 1108-1516; Proceedings of the Society of Antiquaries 1876-.

Publications: Local Studies Collection leaflet; inventory of the whole collection; publications list; handlist of Midlothian County Council Archives in the SRO; The prisoners at Penicuik / Ian MacDougall; The Parish of Cockpen in the olden time / Peter Mitchell. - 1881; Facsimile map of Midlothian (1838).

Photocopies: A3, A4. Mfilm/mfiche prints.

138   Milngavie and Bearsden Historical Society

c/o Bearsden and Milngavie Libraries Dept, Brookwood, 166 Drymen Road, BEARSDEN G61 3RJ
Tel.: 041-943 0121
Contact: Ms E Brown (Librarian)

Collection of press cuttings and information on local farms and mills.

Prior consultation advisable.

Mon-Fri 1000-2000; Sat 1000-1700.

In town centre; railway station near; on bus routes; parking.

Primary source material: Original material on local topics and places.

Publications: Glassford of Dougalston / C. Castle.

Photocopies: A4.

139   Monklands District Libraries: Local History Department

Airdrie Library, Wellwynd, AIRDRIE ML6 0AG
Tel.: 0236-63221 7   763221
Contact: Mrs Elaine Clifford

The Local Collection includes general and local historical books and pamphlet material covering places, events & prominent people in the Monklands District. The collection includes maps, photographs & ephemeral material 17thC-.

Prior consultation advisable.

Mon-Tue, Thu-Fri 0930-1930; Sat 0930-1700.

In the town centre near the market place; parking; Airdrie railway station near; bus routes nearby; disabled access to lending library only.

Primary source material: Airdrie & Coatbridge Advertiser 1855- and other local newspapers [mfilm and bound copies]; Airdrie Burgh Town Council minutes 1821-1974, Coatbridge Burgh Town Council minutes 1885-1974 [mfilm and bound copies]; Old Monkland & New Monkland census returns 1811-81 [mfilm]; Airdrie valuation roll 1855-1988, Coatbridge valuation roll 1887-1988 [mfilm and bound copies]; OPRs for Old Monkland & New Monkland pre-1854 [mfilm].

Publications: List of publications; and leaflet detailing services.

Photocopies: A3, A4. Mfilm/fiche prints.

140   **Moray District Council Department of Libraries & Museums: Local Studies Collection**

Elgin Library, Grant Lodge, ELGIN IV30 1HS
Tel.: 0343-542746 Fax: 0343-549050
Contact: Mr Mike Seton

Collection covers all aspects of life in Moray, past and present. It includes about 8000 books and pamphlets, 14000 photographs and slides and a comprehensive collection of maps. Computer and card indexes (about 0.25 million entries at present) in progress.

Mon-Fri 0930-2000; Sat 1000-1200.

Grant Lodge is in the Cooper Park, east of the town centre and 200 yards west of the Cathedral; bus route nearby; parking.

Primary source material: Newspapers 1747- to date [mfilm]; monumental inscriptions; large collection 19th & 20thC local architects' plans; census enumeration books 1841-81 [mfilm]; OPRs 1609-1854 [mfilm]; valuation rolls 1855-1989 (gaps); poor relief, school and burial ground records [mfilm]; collection of miscellaneous archival and MS records; file of newspaper cuttings.

Publications: Tracing your roots in Moray [leaflet].

Photocopies: A3, A4. Mfilm/mfiche prints. Copies of photographs supplied to order.

141 Moray District Council Museums Service

Falconer Museum, Tolbooth Street, FORRES IV36 OPH
Tel.: 0309-73701 Fax: 0309-74166
Contact: The Curator.

Photographic collections covering the district of Moray. Specialised archive collections relating to Hugh Falconer and Peter F. Anson.

Prior consultation advisable.

Mon-Fri 1000-1230, 1330-1630.

The Falconer Museum is situated in Tolbooth St off High St; bus route & parking near; disabled access to the ground floor only.

Primary source material: Archive relating to Hugh Falconer (1808-1865), palaeontologist and Vice President, The Royal Society; archive, paintings and photographs relating to Peter F. Anson (1889-1975), marine artist and author; medieval MS, part of the index to the Chartulary of the Diocese of Moray.

Publications: 20 Museum information sheets on local topics; The so-called Sueno Stone at Forres.

Photocopies: A4 (A3 by arrangement). Photographic copying by prior arrangement.

142 Morningside Heritage Association

c/o S. Smith (Chairman), 32 Swan Spring Avenue, EDINBURGH EH10 6NH
Tel.: 031-445 2527
Contact: S Smith (Chairman)

Primary source material: Interview tapes for Morningside memories publication.

Publications: Morningside memories.

143   **Motherwell District Libraries: Heritage Section**

Motherwell Library, Hamilton Road, MOTHERWELL ML1 3BZ
Tel.: 0698-51311   Fax: 0698-~~54543~~   ~~254543~~ 25(3)(
Contact: Mr Ronald Kelsall (Heritage Librarian)

Collection includes 1000 books about Lanarkshire and Motherwell district in particular. Pamphlets and ephemera, maps, 3000 photographs and slides (indexed), census returns and OPRs [mfilm], newspapers (Motherwell Times 1883- and Wishaw Press 1873-, both indexed, also Motherwell Standard from 1898-1917). SRA DS 6/12.

Prior consultation advisable.

Mon-Tue, Thu-Fri 0900-1900; Wed 0900-1200; Sat 0900-1700.

Railway station near; parking nearby (behind Old Town Hall); disabled access to library but not to local collection.

Primary source material: Letter books of Motherwell Burgh and Wishaw Burgh; minute books of local co-operative and other societies (Wishaw 1890-1955); Lord Hamilton of Dalzell collection of family documents and letters from 17th-19thC; Hurst Nelson & Co. Ltd collection of photographs of railway, rolling stock, trams, etc. (indexed); census returns of Bothwell, Dalziel, Cambusnethan, Hamilton & Shotts, all 1841-81 with part coverage of many surrounding parishes [mfilm]; OPRs of Bothwell, Cambusnethan, Dalserf, Dalziel, Shotts and Hamilton [mfilm]; Dolphinton (births and marriages only).

Publications: List of publications.

Photocopies: A3, A4. Mfilm/mfiche prints: A4. Photographic prints may be ordered.

144   **Mull Museum Association**

Columba Buildings, TOBERMORY PA75 6NY

MS, photographic records, maps & plans; reference library covering Mull and some West Highland areas & islands.

Prior consultation advisable, in writing. Admission: 50p adult; 10p under 16 years; membership £2.00 pa.

Mon-Fri 1030-1630; Sat 1030-1300 (Easter-mid Oct).

In Tobermory village; car parking nearby.

Primary source material: MS, copied MS and printed materials covering aspects of life in Mull and other islands, including maps and plans; artifacts, photographs and information on the galleon sunk in Tobermory Bay 1588.

145 Nairn Literary Institute

c/o Nairn Library, 68 High Street, NAIRN IV12 4AU
Tel.: 0667-52367 Fax: 0667-52443
Contact: Miss Somerville (Librarian); Mr A McGowan (Hon. Librarian)
Contact's address: c/o Nairn Literary Institute, Viewfield House, Nairn (Hon. Librarian).

Extensive collection of historical books with most published in 19th and early 20thC including Spalding Club publications, covering the Church in Scotland, social history, travel in Scotland, biography and genealogy, northern and north central Scotland.

Visitors by appointment.

Mon 1400-2000; Tue 1400-1800; Wed, Sat 1000-1300; Thu 1000-1800; Fri 1000-2000.

In centre of town; bus station & parking at rear; disabled access.

Primary source material: Nairnshire Telegraph 1855- [mfilm]; IGI.

Publications: Teens and twenties (reminiscences of Nairn).

Photocopies: A3, A4.

146 National Gallery of Scotland: Library

The Mound, EDINBURGH EH2 2FL
Tel.: 031-556 8921 x214 Fax: 031-220 0917
Contact: Mrs Julia Rolfe

NB This is a private working library; access to archival material or books by members of the public is dependant on them not being available in any other library in Edinburgh. Check with the Union Catalogue of Art Books in Edinburgh (UCABEL) in the NLS before contacting the National Gallery of Scotland Library.

Visitors by appointment.

Mon-Fri 1000-1230, 1400-1630 (subject to the availability of the librarian).

The National Gallery is behind the Royal Scottish Academy at the halfway point of Princes St; Waverley railway station 0.25 miles; St Andrews Square bus station 0.5 miles; on bus routes; short stay parking near, long stay 0.5 miles; disabled access and adjacent parking.

Primary source material: Books, periodicals and exhibition catalogues on Western art, particularly as related to the gallery's own collection of paintings; files on the gallery's collection of paintings; photographs of paintingss in other collections both private and public; collection of miscellaneous archival and MS records; press cuttings relating to the gallery.

Limited photocopying.

147   National Library of Scotland: Main Library

George 1V Bridge, EDINBURGH EH1 1EW
Tel.: 031-226 4531   Fax: 031-220 6662
Contact: Information desk staff.

The National Library of Scotland is Scotland's largest library with some 5 million printed books and pamphlets and around 70,000 volumes of MS. Special emphasis is given to all aspects of Scottish history, life and culture.   The library's reading rooms are for reference and research that cannot easily be carried out elsewhere, and admission to them is by reader's ticket (application forms are available from the Superintendent of Readers' Services).

Prior consultation advisable.

Mon-Tue, Thu-Fri 0930-2030; Wed 1000-2030; Sat 0930-1300.

City centre location; Waverley railway station 0.25 miles; St Andrew Square bus station 0.5 miles; on city bus routes; short stay parking nearby, long stay 0.5 miles; disabled access (bell at door).

Primary source material: See National Library of Scotland: Manuscripts Division.

Publications: Information pack available from the library shop.

*Photocopies: A0, A1, A2, A3, A4 (b&w); A3, A4 (col).
Mfilm/mfiche prints. Full photographic service.*

148   National Library of Scotland: Manuscripts Division

George 1V Bridge, EDINBURGH EH1 1EW
Tel.: 031-226 4531 x2314   Fax: 031-220 6662
Contact: Keeper: Manuscripts, Maps & Music.

The Manuscript Division houses a very large collection, mostly relating to Scots and Scotland (c30,000 volumes fully catalogued, 30,000+ less thoroughly listed).

Prior consultation advisable. MS enquiries x2319/2113. Latest time for orders 1630.

Mon-Tue, Thu-Fri 0930-2015; Wed 1000-2015; Sat 0930-1300.

South Reading Room is in the National Library of Scotland: Main Library (qv).

Primary source material: Papers of a wide variety of individuals, families, estates, organisations relating to many different areas, including correspondence, legal, financial and estate papers, maps and plans, photographs, journals.

Publications: National Library of Scotland: Catalogue of manuscripts acquired since 1925, vols.1-7. - 1938-89; further vols. in preparation (may be consulted in the library). Inventories of other collections available in the library or in mfiche in the National Inventory of Documentary Sources (UK). Main accessions mentioned in the library's Annual Report and in the Historical Manuscripts Commission's List of accessions to repositories.

Photocopies: A0, A1, A2, A3, A4 (b&w); A3, A4 (col).
Mfilm/mfiche prints. Full photographic service.

149   National Library of Scotland: Map Library

Causewayside Building, 33 Salisbury Place, EDINBURGH EH9 1SL
Tel.: 031-226 4531   Fax: 031-668 3472
Contact: Ms Margaret Wilkes (Head of Map Library); Mrs Diana Webster (Map Library Manager)
Contacts' tel.nos.: x3411 (Head of Map Library); x3413/3412 (Map Library manager).

The Map Library, for reference only, has some 1.5 million cartographic items (both early and modern) including maps, charts, plans, atlases, gazetteers and cartographic reference books for all parts of the world. It is particularly strong in maps and atlases with a Scottish association, i.e. compiled, engraved, published or printed in Scotland, but relating to all engraved, published or printed in Scotland, but relating to all parts of the world, as well as foreign published maps of those parts of the world where Scots have explored, travelled, settled or been involved. There is a comprehensive collection of printed maps of the whole or parts of Scotland 16th-20thC. There are some general reference books including the Statistical Accounts to allow better understanding of the map collection.

Visitors by appointment only if request is complex or requires much pre-1800 material. Handling charges apply for bulk photography orders or 'fast' service.

Mon-Tue, Thu-Fri 0930-1700; Wed 1000-1700; Sat 0930-1300. Last maps retrieved from stacks Mon-Fri 1630, Sat 1230.

Map Library (map reference NT 264721) is at junction of Causewayside and Grange/Salisbury roads, 1 mile due south of Princes St and Waverley station; 1.25 miles from St Andrew Square bus station; bus routes nearby; limited parking in immediate area; disabled access, please telephone in advance of visit.

Primary source material: OS maps at all scales 1801- with comprehensive coverage of Scotland; other topographic and thematic maps at medium and small scales; official British-produced sea charts.

Publications: Map Library leaflets. Publications are included in NLS catalogue of publications.

Photocopies: A0, A1, A2, A3, A4 (b&w); A3, A4 (col). Mfilm/mfiche prints. Full photographic service. Subject to copyright restrictions.

150   National Monuments Record of Scotland

6/7 Coates Place, EDINBURGH EH3 7AA
Tel.: 031-225 5994 Fax: 031-220 6581
Contact: Dr Graham Ritchie

This library is maintained by the Royal Commission on the Ancient and Historical Mouments of Scotland and houses a comprehensive collection of prints and drawings, photographs, MS, books, maps amd ephemera relating to Scottish archaeology, architecture and industrial archaeology. 14000 books include a large and growing collection of topographical books, Scottish history and periodicals.

Visitors by appointment. Prior consultation advisable to find out if material is available on specific subjects.

Mon-Thu 0930-1300, 1400-1630; Fri 0930-1300, 1400-1600.

Between Haymarket and the West End; Haymarket railway station 400 yards; on bus routes; parking near. NB Moving to Bernard Terrace off Clerk St, early 1992; 1 mile south of G.P.O. in Princes St; on bus routes; parking nearby; disabled access.

Primary source material: Prints and Drawings Collections including office collections of major Scottish architcts (William Burn, Dunn and Findlay, Thoms and Wilkie, Dundee); measured surveys drawn from RCAHMS field surveys, covering building, industrial archaeology and archaeology; photographs acquired from RCAHMS field surveys, aerial photographs from current flying programme, vertical aerial photographs dating from the late 1940s and 50s; antiquarian photographs including the Rokeby collection of railway photographs; MS range from 18thC architects' contracts, research material compiled for government and other reports (e.g. Scottish Burgh Survey, excavation reports to papers on plasterers and decorative woodworkers); OS name book [mfilm].

Publications: National Monuments Record of Scotland Jubilee; Guide to the collections, May 1991; User guide; RCAHMS leaflet.

Photocopies: A3, A4. Photographic prints from negatives. Mfilm & mfiche prints. Dyeline and triplex copies of plans where applicable.

151   National Museums of Scotland: Library

Chambers Street, EDINBURGH EH1 1JF
Tel.: 031-225 7534 x153/269/271   Fax: 031-220 4819
Contact: Any member of Library staff.

Books on Scottish industrial archaeology and technology, natural history and geology are included in the collection, also biographies of Scottish scientists.

Visitors by appointment.

Mon-Thu 1000-1230, 1400-1700; Fri 1000-1230, 1400-1630.

Library located in the Royal Museum of Scotland; Waverley railway station 0.5 miles; St Andrew Square Bus Station 0.75 miles; bus routes nearby; parking; disabled access to museum at rear, difficult access to library.

Primary source material: Archival material, MS letters, notebooks, etc., belonging to J A Harvie-Brown, William Jardine and William Bruce, handlists of which were published in the Royal Scottish Museum information series: natural history, nos.7-9.

Publications: NMS publications list.

Photocopies: A3, A4.

152 National Museums of Scotland: Library

Queen Street, EDINBURGH EH2 1JD
Tel.: 031-225 7534 x369/375 Fax: 031-557 9498
Contact: The Librarian.

Extensive Scottish archaeological collection; Scottish history and topography, family histories, in monograph and journal. Much 18th, 19th and early 20thC material.

Mon-Fri 1000-1230, 1330-1700.

East end of Queen St; Waverley railway station near; St Andrew Square Bus Station and parking nearby; disabled access.

Primary source material: Acts of Parliament of Scotland; Exchequer Rolls; MS records of Society of Antiquaries of Scotland; miscellaneous MS.

Publications: NMS publications list.

Photocopies: A3, A4. Mfiche prints. Photographic service available.

153 National Museums of Scotland: Museum of Flight

East Fortune Airfield, NORTH BERWICK EH39 5LE
Tel.: 0620-88308
Contact: Mr Colin Hendry; Sqn Ldr R J Major

Small library contains a wide range of general aviation publications, periodicals, documents, photographs, manuals, log books and maps. Much of the material concerns East Fortune Airfield itself and aviation in the locality.

Visitors by appointment, Mon-Fri 1030-1500 (Oct-Easter).

Sun-Sat 1030-1630 (Easter-Sep).

East Fortune Airfield lies 20 miles east of Edinburgh, 2 miles along the B1347 (2 miles east of Haddington on the A1); not served by public transport; parking; disabled access.

Primary source material: Comprehensive airship histories with regard to local area (World War I RNAS East coast patrols); original drawings for the R34; periodicals including Aero 1909-10, Aeroplane Spotter World War II, and various station magazines; 603 (City of Edinburgh) Squadron material; spread of technical manuals from light aircraft to Avro Vulcan.

Publications: General information leaflet. Index list of publications and subjects covered.

Photocopies: A3, A4 (available via NMS Chambers St, Edinburgh).

154   National Museums of Scotland: Scottish Ethnological Archive

York Buildings, Queen Street, EDINBURGH EH2 1JD
Tel.: 031-225 7534 x303   Fax: 031-220 4819
Contact: Ms Dorothy I Kidd (Curator)

The Scottish Ethnological Archive is organised by subject. Material dates from 17thC and includes photographs, slides, postcards, trade catalogues, maps, plans, videos and oral recordings, articles, newspaper cuttings, bibliographical references and references to original material held elsewhere, together with a medium-sized collection of miscellaneous MS records and printed ephemera. The Archive is an invaluable resource for the study of Scotland's material culture.

Visitors by appointment. Charges made for commercial searches.

Mon-Fri 0930-1700.

York Buildings, east end of Queen St, opposite Royal Museum and Scottish National Portrait Gallery; Waverley railway station near; St Andrew Square Bus Station and parking nearby; disabled access difficult.

Primary source material: Other than a very large collection of original prints and negatives the primary source material is limited in size. It includes farm diaries; tradesmen's day books and account books; wills and inventories; the archives of the firms of Macfarlan and Shearer of Greenock and T Sheriff of West Barns, East Lothian; MS recipe books; miscellaneous MS material and a collection of printed ephemera.

Publications: The Scottish Ethnological Archive (guide and subject index); lists of the large trade catalogue collection; list of small agricultural video collection; list of tape recorded interviews.

Photocopies: A3, A4. Photographs: 5x7"-16x20".

155 National Museums of Scotland: Scottish United Services Museum

The Castle, EDINBURGH EH1 2NG
Tel.: 031-225 7534 x404
Contact: Ms Ruth E Wilson (Librarian)

Scottish military history including navy & RAF 1660-; limited biographical information in official Army lists; Scottish regimental histories and journals; print collection of the Department of Armed Forces History may be consulted by appointment only.

Visitors by appointment. Admission charge to the Castle.

Mon-Fri 0930-1230, 1400-1700.

In Edinburgh Castle; Waverley railway station 0.5 miles; St Andrew Square Bus Station 0.75 miles; bus routes near; parking nearby; disabled access by special arrangement.

Primary source material: MS relating to regiments including some order books; letters and diaries including papers of Sir David Baird; Duke of Cumberland's papers [mfilm].

Photocopies: A3, A4.

156 The National Trust for Scotland

5 Charlotte Square, EDINBURGH EH2 4DU
Tel.: 031-226 5922 Fax: 031-220 6266

Properties with book collections include: Barrie's Birthplace; Brodick Castle; Brodie Castle; Carlyle's Birthplace; Drum Castle; Fyvie Castle; Haddo House; Hill of Tarvit; Hugh Miller's Cottage and Leith Hall.

Visitors by appointment (refer to the Trust's annual Guide to properties and contact The Representative for individual properties).

For opening hours and locations refer to the Guide to properties.

Primary source material: Some collections have a small quantity of MS (ask Representative for information).

Publications: Guide to properties [annual].

157   The Natural History & Antiquarian Society of Mid Argyll

c/o Fiona MacDonald (Hon. Secretary), 9 Cairnbaan Cottages, Cairnbaan, LOCHGILPHEAD PA31 8SJ
Contact: Ms Fiona MacDonald (Hon Secretary)

Reports, etc. by members on local archaeological finds and excavations, some of which featured in the Society's publication Kist.

Visitors by appointment.

Publications: Kist (twice yearly); Mid Argyll archaeological guide / M. Campbell; Wayside sketches and favourite views / Dr. F.S. McKenna; Solar alignment at Brainport Bay, Minard / Col. P. Gladwin.

158   North East Fife District Library Service: The Hay Fleming Reference Library

St Andrews Library, Church Square, ST ANDREWS KY16 9NN
Tel.: 0334-73381
Contact: Branch Librarian.

The Hay Fleming Reference Library incorporates material on Scottish history, religion, literature and a comprehensive collection on St Andrews (guide books, pamphlets, press cuttings, photographs and books).

Family history search fee, telephone & post: £6.00.

Mon-Wed, Fri 1000-1900; Thu, Sat 1000-1700.

In town centre, off South St; bus station and long term parking near.

Primary source material: St Andrews Citizen 1873-1990 [mfilm]; MS records on local trades and churches; MS notebooks of Dr Hay Fleming's research.

Photocopies: A3, A4. Reproductions of photographs can be arranged.

159 **North East Fife District Library Service: Local History Collection**

Cupar Library, Crossgate, CUPAR KY15 5AS
Tel.: 0334-53001
Contact: Branch Librarian.

Books, pamphlets, periodicals, newspapers, press cuttings, maps, prints, photographs on Fife generally and North East Fife in particular.

Prior consultation advisable. Family history search fee, telephone & post: £6.00.

Mon-Wed, Fri 1000-1900; Thu, Sat 1000-1700.

In town centre; bus routes, railway station & parking nearby.

Primary source material: Census enumeration records 1841-1881 [mfilm]; OPRs 1650-1854 [mfilm]; IGI; register of sasines; Fifeshire Journal 1833-93 [mfilm]; East Fife Record [mfilm].

Publications: Leaflets: Local history collection, Family history.

Photocopies: A3, A4. Mfilm prints: A4. Reproductions of photographs can be arranged.

160 **North East Fife District Museum Service**

County Buildings, St Catherine Street, CUPAR
Tel.: 0334-53722 x141
Contact: Ms Gillian Wilson

Maps, plans, photographs, postcards and printed ephemera of the Fife area plus a small collection of MS material.

Visitors by appointment.

Mon-Fri 0900-1700.

In town centre; bus routes, railway station, parking nearby; disabled access.

Primary source material: Records and correspondence of the Newburgh Friendly Society and the Anderson family of Newburgh.

Photocopies: A3, A4. Photographic service.

161   North East Fife District Museum Service: Laing Museum & Library

High Street, NEWBURGH
Contact: Ms Gillian Wilson
Contact's tel.no.: 0334-53722 x141.

Comprehensive collection of books on Scottish history and archaeology with particular reference to Fife.

Prior consultation advisable.

Mon-Fri 1100-1800; Sat-Sun 1400-1700 (Apr-Sep); Wed-Thu 1200-1600; Sun 1400-1700 (Oct-Mar).

In town centre; on bus route; parking nearby.

162   North East of Scotland Library Service: Ellon Library

Station Road, ELLON AB41 9AZ
Tel.: 0358-20865
Contact: Mr D Watson

Books, maps, photographs and other material of relevance to Ellon and its surrounding area.

Prior consultation advisable.

Mon-Fri 1000-1300, 1400-1930; Sat 1000-1230, 1330-1600.

Close to town centre; on bus route; parking; disabled access.

Primary source material: OPRs and census records 1841-81 for Ellon and surrounding parishes [mfilm]; IGI(S) 1988 [mfiche]; Ellon and District Advertiser 1957- [mfilm].

Photocopies: A3, A4.

163   North East of Scotland Library Service: Fraserburgh Library

King Edward Street, FRASERBURGH AB5 5PN
Tel.: 0346-28197
Contact: Mr D Catto

Books, photographs, maps and other material relating to Fraserburgh and its surrounding area.

Prior consultation advisable.

Mon-Wed, Fri 0930-1900; Thu 0930-1700; Sat 1000-1300, 1400-1700.

In west end of the town; on bus route; on-street parking.

Primary source material: Fraserburgh Advertiser 1858-1941 (with gaps) [mfilm]; Fraserburgh Herald 1884- [mfilm and bound]; OPRs and census records for all of Banff and Buchan District 1848-1881; IGI(BI) 1988.

Photocopies: A3, A4. Mfilm/mfiche prints: A4.

164 North East of Scotland Library Service: Huntly Library

The Square, HUNTLY AB5 5BR
Tel.: 0466-2179
Contact: Mr D Watson
Contact's tel.no.: 0358-20865.

Books and other materials of relevance to Huntly and the surrounding area.

Prior consultation advisable.

Mon, Thu 1430-1700; Tue, Fri 1430-1930; Wed 1030-1230, 1430-1930; Sat 1030-1230, 1400-1600.

In town square; railway station 0.75 miles; bus route nearby; on-street parking.

Primary source material: OPRs and census records for surrounding parishes 1841-1881 [mfilm]; IGI(S) 1984 [mfiche]; Huntly Express 1864- [bound & mfilm]; George MacDonald Collection of books, letters and other MS material written by, or relating to the novelist George MacDonald.

165 North East of Scotland Library Service: Local History Department

Meldrum Meg Way, Meadows Industrial Estate, OLDMELDRUM AB51 0GN
Tel.: 06512-2707 x17 Fax: 06512-2142
Contact: Miss L Donald

A comprehensive collection of books, maps, photographs, postcards and other material relating to events, people and places in Banff and Buchan, Gordon and Kincardine and Deeside districts.

Visitors by appointment.

Mon-Fri 0900-1700.

The Meadows industrial estate is on the outskirts of the town on the B9170 Oldmeldrum to Inverurie Rd; bus stop is in the Town Square c400 yds from HQ; parking; disabled access.

Primary source material: OPRs [mfilm] and census records 1841-1881 [mfilm] for Banff and Buchan, Gordon and Kincardine & Deeside; IGI(S) 1988, and the county indexes for Aberdeen City, Aberdeenshire, Banffshire and Kincardineshire [mfiche]; local newspapers (list available) [mfilm]; The Strichen Estate Papers [MS] (mfilm copies at Strichen Library).

Publications: Family history leaflet; Holdings of genealogical material on mfilm leaflet; Newspaper holdings leaflet; facsimile maps: Aberdeenshire (1807), Kincardineshire (1822), Banffshire (1826), Buchan (1826). Turriff (1819).

Photocopies: A3, A4. Mfilm/mfiche prints: A4.

166   **North East of Scotland Library Service: Macduff Library**

17 High Street, MACDUFF AB4 1LR
Tel.: 0261-43891
Contact: Mr A J J McNeill

Books and other material of relevance to Macduff and surrounding area.

Prior consultation advisable.

Tue 1500-2000; Wed 1500-1700; Thu 1000-1200, 1800-2000; Sat 1000-1200, 1400-1600.

Near town centre; bus route nearby; on-street parking; disabled access.

Primary source material: Banffshire Journal 1845- [bound & mfilm]; Banffshire Reporter 1869-1920 [mfilm]; OPRs and census records for surrounding parishes 1841-1881; IGI(S) 1984.

Photocopies: A4.

167   North East of Scotland Library Service: Peterhead Library

St Peter Street, PETERHEAD AB4 6QD
Tel.: 0779-72554
Contact: Miss S Allan

Books, photographs and other material relating to Peterhead and its surrounding area.

Prior consultation advisable.

Mon-Tue, Thu-Fri 0930-1900; Wed, Sat 0930-1700.

In town centre; bus station nearby; on-street parking; disabled access.

Primary source material: Peterhead Sentinel 1856-1914, Buchan Observer 1863- [bound & mfilm]; OPRs and census records for Peterhead and surrounding parishes 1841-1881; IGI(S) 1988.

Photocopies: A3, A4. Mfiche/mfilm prints: A4.

168   North East of Scotland Library Service: Stonehaven Library

Evan Street, STONEHAVEN AB3 2ET
Tel.: 0569-62136
Contact: Mrs L Masson

Books, maps and other material relevant to Stonehaven and surrounding area.

Prior consultation advisable.

Mon-Tue 1000-1230, 1430-2000; Wed 1000-1200; Thu-Fri 1430-2000; Sat 1000-1200, 1400-1600.

Near town centre; railway station 0.5 miles; on bus route; on-street parking.

Primary source material: Kincardineshire Observer 1907-, Mearns Leader 1913- [mfilm, 1975- bound]; Stonehaven Journal 1840-1917 [bound & mfilm]; OPRs and census records for surrounding parishes 1841-1881; IGI(S) 1988.

Photocopies: A3, A4.

169   **North East of Scotland Library Service: Strichen Library**

59a Water Street, STRICHEN AB4 4ST
Tel.: 07715-347
Contact: Mr D Catto
Contact's tel.no.: 0346-28197.

Local history collection contains books and other material on Strichen and its surrounding area.

Prior consultation advisable.

Mon, Wed, Fri 1700-1900; Thu 1400-1700; Sat 1000-1200.

Close to centre of village; on bus route; on street parking.

Primary source material: OPRs and census records for Strichen and surrounding parishes 1841-1881 [mfilm]; IGI(S) 1988 [mfilm]; The Strichen Estate Papers [mfilm] (originals are retained at the Local History Department in HQ).

Photocopies: A3, A4. Mform prints: A4.

170   **North East of Scotland Museum Service: Arbuthnot Museum**

St Peter Street, PETERHEAD AB42 6QD
Tel.: 0779-77778
Contact: Miss J Chamberlain-Mole (Curator); Dr David Bertie (Depute Curator)

Photographic collection & whaling records.

Prior consultation advisable; donations welcomed.

Mon-Sat 1000-1200, 1400-1700 (Fri, if professional help needed).

Town centre; parking nearby.

Primary source material: Large local photographic collection 1890-; museum displays; some MS records of whaling; James Ferguson artifacts, some printed.

Photocopies: A3, A4. Photographs up to 16x12".

171   Northern College of Education Library Service

Aberdeen Campus, Hilton Place, ABERDEEN AB9 1FA
Tel.: 0224-283571 Fax: 0224-497046
Contact: Miss Jean Jolly (Senior Librarian (User Services)); Mr
G C K Smith-Burnett (Principal Librarian, Archival Material)
Contacts' tel.nos.: 0224-283570 (User Services); -283568 (Archival
Material).

Local history collection includes books, pamphlets and some periodicals relating to Aberdeen City and Grampian Region. Maps and plans of Aberdeen and environs in map collection. Primary source material in reserve collection.

Prior consultation advisable.

Mon-Fri 0900-2130; Sat 0930-1230 (term); Mon-Fri 0900-1700 (vacation).

Main library is in main college building 1.5 miles north west of city centre; railway station and bus routes nearby; parking on campus; disabled access by arrangement.

Primary source material: Aberdeen Church of Scotland Training College records of classes 1874/5-1905/7, registers of marks 1896/7-1900/1, registers of students 1874-1906, various results, reports, documents, press cuttings 1887-1905; Aberdeen United Free Church Training College registers of marks 1890/5-1906/7, teaching practice record books 1876-1906/8; Aberdeen Training Centre register of students admitted 1906-49, register of students admitted under Chapter V 1907-50, register of students admitted under Chapter VI 1907-49, register of marks 1910-48, minutes of meetings (Aberdeen Provincial Committee) 1905-59, photographs of principals, lecturers & students 1875-1949, press cuttings 1909-59, cuttings of job advertisements 1913-66; Aberdeen College of Education minutes of meetings 1962-87, quadrennial reports 1967/71-1979/83, triennial report 1964/67; Aberdeen T.C. (later College of Education) Demonstration School admission register 1934-68, register of leavers 1925-70, summary registers 1967-70, daily register 1952-57, 1968-70, log books 1888-1970, record books & miscellaneous papers 1846-1970, register of admission, etc. 1909-34.

Publications: Guide to library services (Aberdeen Library).

Photocopies: A3, A4.

172   Orkney Library & Archives

Laing Street, KIRKWALL KW15 1NW
Tel.: 0856-3166
*Contact: Mr Robert Tulloch (Chief Librarian); Ms Alison Fraser
(Archivist); Mr David Mackie (Photography Archivist); Ms Ann
Manson (Sound Archivist)*

**Local History Collection includes 2900 books, 1200 pamphlets,
local newspapers Orcadian (since 1854) and Orkney Herald
(1861-1961). Extensive archive collection includes most of The
Scottish Record Office Orkney material on mfiche and a large
photographic and sound archive. SRA DS 6/2.**

*Prior consultation advisable. Archives by appointment only
(Mon-Tue, Thu-Fri 0900-1300, 1400-1700).*

Mon-Fri 0900-2000; Sat 0900-1700.

Off main street; parking near; disabled access.

**Primary source material: Large collection of books on Orkney
1503-; census material; parish & church records; Sheriff Court
records; valuation rolls; sasines; business records; private
papers. The Photographic Archive comprises 16000 negatives
covering all aspects of Orkney life 1870-. The Sound Archive
has an extensive collection of oral history tapes of people and
music.**

Photocopies: A3, A4. Limited photographic service.

173   **Paisley College Library**

High Street, PAISLEY PA1 2BE
Tel.: 041-848 3759 Fax: 041-887 0812
*Contact: The Librarian (041-848 3750); Depute Librarian
(Technical Services) (041-848 3763).*

**The College Library maintains a small collection of books and
some other materials relating to the history of Paisley,
Renfrewshire and the West of Scotland.**

Visitors by appointment (contact Miss S Macpherson 041-848 3758).

**Mon-Fri 0900-2100; Sat 0900-1700 (term); Mon-Fri 0900-1700
(vacation).**

Paisley College is opposite Paisley Central Library; Gilmour St railway station near; main bus routes nearby; parking; disabled access but please contact library first.

Primary source material: Collection of railway maps salvaged from St Enoch's Station; Paisley and Renfrewshire Standard 1869-71, Paisley Advertiser 1824-27, 1842-44 and Renfrewshire Advertiser 1848-50 [mfilm]; some census data [mfilm].

Publications: Calendar of railway documents (available for reference in the College Library and copies on deposit in other Scottish libraries).

Photocopies: A3, A4. Mfilm/mfiche prints. Photographic services available by arrangement.

Council

174 **Perth and Kinross ~~District~~ Libraries: Local Studies Collection**

The Sandeman Library, 16 Kinnoull Street, PERTH PH1 5ET
Tel.: ~~0738-23320~~ Fax: ~~0738-36364~~ 01738 – 477062
Contact: J Duncan (Local Studies Librarian); S Connelly (Archivist)

Local Studies Collection includes some 9000 books and 3000 pamphlets on Perth and district, plus books printed and published in the area; bibliographies; local directories 1837-; newspapers; maps; together with the District Archive's MS material. SRA DS 6/19.

Visitors by appointment for Archives. Search charge for enquirers living outwith District: £5 per hour.

Mon-Wed 0930-1700; Thu-Fri 0930-2000; Sat 0900-1300.

Central Perth; bus routes & parking nearby; railway station 0.5 miles; some materials can be taken to a separate library for the disabled nearby.

Primary source material: Athol music collection [MS]; eight newspapers, the oldest dating from 1809 with incomplete indexes for most of them; census and OPRs [mfilm]; 50 early maps and plans for Perthshire and Perth 1715-1900 plus OS maps; the OS Archaeological Records card index, and reports of the Scottish Archaeological Trust covering the area; the District Archive holding local authority records prior to 1975, including City and Royal Burgh of Perth 14th-20thC small Burghs mainly 19th-20thC, and the Counties of Perth and Kinross 17th-20thC.

Publications: Sources of information for local studies 1989; Annals of Auchterarder / A.G. Reid; Tales of Rannoch / A.D. Cunningham; Alert all clear; John Pullar & Sons Ltd / A.W. Harding; A short list of Perth flooers & beasties (Scots education pack).

Photocopies: A3, A4.

175   Perth Museum and Art Gallery

George Street, PERTH PH1 5LB
Tel.: 0738-32488 x17 Fax: 0738-35225
Contact: Ms Susan Payne (Keeper of Human History)

Social history, archives, photographs, numismatics, archaeology, fine and applied art and natural history. In the main these cover the history of Perth and Kinross District. SRA DS 6/21.

Visitors by appointment.

Mon-Sat 1000-1700.

At top of George St near Perth Bridge; within walking distance of railway and bus stations; parking; disabled people can be catered for with prior notice.

Primary source material: c200000 negatives with views of Perth and Perthshire c1860-; archives relating to the history of Perth Museum, the Perthshire Society for Natural Science and the Literary and Antiquarian Society of Perth; some local trades material (e.g. Wrights Incorporation c1680-1921) [mostly MS]; small collection of maps and plans; topographical views of the district; portraits of local people and works by local artists, etc.

Publications: Archives are listed with NRA(S) in Edinburgh; negatives 1860-1930 are listed with NMR, Edinburgh; Catalogue of the permanent collection of paintings and drawings.

Photocopies: A4. Photographic services including mfilm, details on request.

176   Queen's Own Highlanders: Regimental Archives

Cameron Barracks, Old Perth Road, INVERNESS IV2 3XZ
Tel.: 0463-224380
Contact: The Regimental Secretary.

Regimental records, photos, publications, documents. Does not include personal records which are held by Public Records Office, Army Records Office, London.

Visitors by appointment.

Mon-Fri 0900-1700.

Cameron Barracks are 1 mile east of the town centre; bus route near; parking; disabled access difficult, contact in advance.

Primary source material: Photo albums; photo files; MS diaries; regimental records; letters; some enlistment books; published histories of 72nd, 78th, 79th Highlanders, Seaforth Highlanders, Cameron Highlanders, Lovat Scouts, Ross Militia, Inverness Militia.

Photocopies: A4.

177   Renfrew District Council. Department of Arts and Libraries: ⟶ MUSEUMS
~~Local History Department~~
PAISLEY MUSEUM
~~Central Library~~, High Street, PAISLEY ~~PA1 2BB~~
Tel.: 041-~~887 3672~~ 889 - 3151   GILLIAN TAIT
Contact: ~~Mr Ken Hinshalwood (Local History Librarian)~~

Locally published books; newspapers; extensive photograph collection; maps; films and videos; genealogical material; local authority records; ephemera; The Paisley Burns Club Collection.

Visitors by appointment for archival items, Mon-Fri 1000-1700 (and to ascertain if material wanted is held).

Mon-Fri 0900-2000; Sat 0900-1700.

The Central Library is opposite Paisley College; Gilmour St railway station near; main bus routes and parking nearby.

Primary source material: Local authority minutes; Paisley Poor Law Records; ephermera material including church magazines and operatic society concert programmes; local newspapers 1824-; several society minute books; MS of locally published works; Cairn of Lochwinnoch c1827-1854; Craigend Papers; Robert Watt's Biblotheca Brittanica; OPRs and census material for Renfrewshire 1841-; extensive coverage of the Paisley shawl industry and some of the large industrial concerns of the area.

Photocopies: A3, A4. Mfilm/mfiche prints: A4.

178   Rowett Research Institute: Reid Library

Greenburn Road, Bucksburn, ABERDEEN AB2 9SB
Tel.: 0224-712751 x336
Contact: Officer-in-charge Library.

A small collection of books and journals published in the 18th & 19thC formerly in the libraries of Sir Archibald Grant of Monymusk, Collingwood Lindsay Wood of Freeland and others. The 120 books and 13 journal titles cover land improvement, animal husbandry, forestry and gardening.

Visitors by appointment.

Mon-Fri 0900-1300, 1400-1600.

6 miles north west of Aberdeen, off A96; bus routes 10 mins walk; parking.

Photocopies: A3, A4.

179   Roxburgh District Museums Service: Hawick Museum

Wilton Lodge, Park, HAWICK TD9 7JL
Tel.: 0450-73457 Fax: 0450-78526
Contact: Ms Rosi Capper

Good library collection (given by Hawick Archaeological Society) of Border history with a good Hawick collection of articles, various journals, newspapers, guidebooks and ephemera plus an extensive archival collection, maps, plans and photographs.

Visitors by appointment. First 0.5 hours free, scaled charges.

Mon-Sat 1000-1200, 1300-1700; Sun 1400-1700 (Apr-Oct); Mon-Fri 1300-1600, Sun 1400-1600 (Nov-Mar).

0.75 miles from the town centre; parking nearby; access for disabled limited to ground floor.

Primary source material: The photographic archive including 19th & 20thC prints, glass negatives and slides; comprehensive monumental inscriptions listings of most Roxburghshire graveyards; local estate, church and farming papers; knitwear archive including local hosiery records; motor vehicle licencing records (Roxburghshire); maps and plans including some 16thC MS pertaining to Mary Queen of Scots; Roxburgh copy of the National Covenant 1638; site records, photographic archive of many local archaeological excavations; miscellaneous MS relating to Hawick Common Riding, Kelso Trades; local newspapers, the Hawick Express and Hawick News late 19thC- [bound vols.]; family history papers, genealogical MS, etc.

Publications: A history of Wilton Lodge; various local history titles; guidebooks for the two Jedburgh museums & the Kelso museum; Mary Queen of Scots literature, including Mary Queen of Scots in Jedburgh 1566; list of hosiery records.

Photocopies: A3, A4. Photographic services available.

180   Royal Botanic Garden Library

Inverleith Row, EDINBURGH EH3 5LR
Tel.: 031-552 7171 Fax: 031-552 0382
Contact: Chief Librarian.

Historical archives on botany, gardening and plant collecting.

Visitors by appointment.

Mon-Thu 0900-1700; Fri 0900-1630.

Within Herbarium Building, Inverleith Row; 1.25 miles north of Princes St; on bus routes; parking nearby.

Primary source material: Historical archives on botany, gardening, plant collecting, etc., including correspondence, diaries, field notebooks, biographical material, photographs [MS].

Photocopies: A4.

181 **Royal College of Physicians & Surgeons: Library**

234 St Vincent Street, GLASGOW G2 5RJ
Tel.: 041-221 6072 Fax: 041-221 1804
Contact: Mr Alex M Rodger; Miss Elizabeth Wilson

College records and examination registers; Macewen Collection (surgery); Ross Collection (tropical medicine); transactions of Glasgow Medical Societies.

Visitors by appointment.

Mon-Fri 0930-1700.

In city centre; Central railway station near; Queen St railway station and bus station 0.5 miles; on bus routes; on-street parking difficult.

Primary source material: Documents and MS of College records; Macewen and Ross Collections detailed in the Archive catalogue.

Publications: Archive catalogue available for inspection only.

Photocopies: A3, A4. Photographs by arrangement.

182 **Royal College of Physicians of Edinburgh: Library**

9 Queen Street, EDINBURGH EH2 1JQ
Tel.: 031-225 7324 x222 Fax: 031-220 3939
Contact: Miss Joan P S Ferguson (Librarian)

Extensive collection of printed books & MS material 15thC-concerning the history of medical science, education and practice, including related topics such as botany.

Visitors by appointment. Donations welcome.

Mon-Fri 0900-1700.

College is midway between North Saint David St and Hanover St; Waverley railway station 0.5 miles; St Andrew Square bus station near; on bus routes; parking near.

Primary source material: Archives of the college including minutes and correspondence; notes of lectures given by founders of the Edinburgh Medical School; case books, correspondence, diaries and other material belonging to medical practitioners; Edinburgh Medical and Surgical Journal 1805- and other periodicals; many portraits and prints of eminent medical men.

Publications: Library leaflet; booklet on the College; photocopies of sections of Catalogue of Printed Books or MS Catalogue; photocopies of detailed listings of selected MS collections.

Photocopies: A3, A4. Photographic slides of portraits.

183   Royal Faculty of Procurators: Library

12 Nelson Mandela Place, GLASGOW G2 1BT
Tel.: 041-332 3593
Contact: Mr Edward M Peirce (Librarian)

The Hill Collection contains a wide-ranging selection of books, journals, maps, plans, newspaper cuttings and other documents primarily relating to the inhabitants of Glasgow and the West of Scotland. It consists of material collected by Dr William Henry Hill up to the year 1912.

Visitors by appointment.

Mon-Fri 0900-1200, 1400-1700.

Nelson Mandela Place (formerly St George Place) is in the city centre; Queen St & Central railway stations near; on bus routes; parking difficult.

Primary source material: Hill munimenta 1520-1897 and genealogical MS relating to this old Glasgow family; Hutcheson papers, original MS including personal papers relating to George & Thomas Hutcheson and Mrs Marion Stewart or Hutcheson; Macfarlane Charters and Writs, original MS relating to the Clan and its Chiefs 1395-1736.

Photocopies: A3, A4.

184   Royal Highland and Agricultural Society of Scotland: Library

Edinburgh Exhibition and Trade Centre, Ingliston, EDINBURGH EH28 8NF
Tel.: 031-333 2444   Fax: 031-333 5326
Contact: The Librarian.

The library houses a collection of c5000 books on agriculture and related subjects.

Visitors by appointment.

Mon-Fri 1000-1600.

Library is in the office building within the Society's Showground with road access off the A8 Glasgow Rd; public transport on A8; parking.

Primary source material: Archival material includes reports and minute books showing the development of the Society since 1784.

Publications: Transactions of the Society to 1968. Annual Show guide and review.

Photocopies: A4.

185 The Royal Highland Fusiliers Regimental Museum

518 Sauchiehall Street, GLASGOW G2 3LW
Tel.: 041-332 0961
Contact: Major W Shaw MBE

The library has a comprehensive collection of books, documents, photographs, regimental histories, scrap books and archival material.

Prior consultation advisable.

Mon-Thu 0830-1630; Fri 0830-1600.

At Charing Cross end of Sauchiehall St; Central, Queen St railway stations and bus station 0.75 miles; on bus routes; parking nearby; disabled access.

Primary source material: Archives and regimental records of the Royal Scots Fusiliers and Highland Light Infantry.

Publications: Museum leaflet.

186 The Royal Scots Regimental Museum Library

The Castle, EDINBURGH EH1 2YT
Tel.: 031-336 1761 x4267
Contact: Lt Col Wilson Smith

Publications, histories, records and archives of the Royal Scots Regiment.

Visitors by appointment to study archives.

Mon-Sat 0930-1630; Sun 1100-1600 (Jun-Oct); Mon-Fri 0930-1600 (Nov-Apr).

Waverley railway station 0.5 miles; St Andrew Square bus station 0.75 miles; bus routes nearby; short-stay parking nearby; disabled access via tunnel.

Primary source material: Archival material including regimental war diaries; rolls of honour (casulties and war graves); regimental record books; copies of training manuals etc., newspaper cuttings.

Publications: NRA(S) 2278 list.

Photocopies: A3, A4.

187   **Royal Scottish Academy Library**

The Mound, EDINBURGH EH2 2EL
Tel.: 031-225 6671   Fax: 031-225 2349
Contact: Mrs Joanna Soden (Assistant Librarian/Keeper)

Local history/studies material is restricted to material connected with the history and working of the Royal Scottish Academy and with painters, sculptors, architects and engravers working in and around Edinburgh, as well as further afield throughout Scotland.

Prior consultation advisable. Donation requested.

Mon-Fri 1000-1300, 1400-1630.

Library entrance is via the rear door of the Academy, which faces the mid point of Princes St, opposite Hanover St; Waverley railway station near; St Andrew Square bus station 0.5 miles; on bus routes; parking near; disabled access.

Primary source material: Complete set of exhibition catalogues of the Royal Scotish Academy Annual Exhibitions 1827-; collection of other catalogues of various art exhibitions held in Edinburgh c1800-; archives including letters written by artists 1827-, documents of art organisations 1729-, and members' files containing photographs, newspapers, cuttings, etc.

Publications: The Royal Scottish Academy 1826-1976 / Esme Gordon; The making of the Royal Scottish Academy / Esme Gordon; James Miller RSA / Lesly Duncan.

Photocopies: A3, A4. Photographs of material can be arranged.

188   Royal Scottish Geographical Society

10 Randolph Crescent, EDINBURGH EH3 7TU
Tel.: 031-225 3330
Contact: A Cruickshank (Secretary)

Major source for 18th & 19thC maps of Scotland, also general library material of Scotland.

Visitors by appointment.

Mon-Fri 1000-1630.

Off Queensferry St (West End); Haymarket railway station 0.5 miles; bus routes and parking nearby; disabled access.

Primary source material: A comprehensive range of early maps of Scotland and OS maps 19thC-.

Publications: Early maps of Scotland (2 vols).

Photocopies: A4.

189   Royal Society of Edinburgh

22-24 George Street, EDINBURGH EH2 2PQ
Tel.: 031-225 6057 Fax: 031-220 6889
Contact: Mrs Tracey Dart; Mr William Brown

The Royal Society of Edinburgh has records of its business dating back to its foundation in 1783. It has a number of MS collections donated mostly by Fellows, the most notable being The Hume Collection. All MS collections are on deposit in the National Library of Scotland Manuscript Division, Edinburgh (qv).

Visitors by appointment. Enquiries by post preferred.

East end of George St, opposite the George Hotel; Waverley railway station, St Andrews Square bus station and bus routes nearby; parking near; disabled access difficult (4 steps).

Primary source material: Society records 1940- (many not available to non-Fellows); older records are on deposit at the NLS; the information mostly concerns individual Fellows and their involvement with the Society.

190 The Scottish Civic Trust

24 George Square, GLASGOW G2 1EF
Tel.: 041-221 1466
Contact: Mr John Gerrard (Technical Director)

Small reference collection relevant particularly to Scotland's built heritage.

Visitors by appointment.

Mon-Fri 0900-1300, 1400-1700.

In city centre; Queen St railway station nearby; Central railway station 0.5 miles; bus station near; on bus routes; on-street parking near.

Primary source material: Complete set of Scottish Development Department lists of buildings of architectural and historic interest; incomplete set of up to date local and structure plans guiding conservation of existing resources and future development; small reference collection of local historical and architectural history material (most of which is otherwise available, e.g. in Mitchell Library); technical publications on conservation of historic buildings; video material on practical building conservation.

Photocopies: A4.

191 The Scottish Film Archive

74 Victoria Crescent Road, GLASGOW G12 9JN
Tel.: 041-334 4445 Fax: 041-334 8132
Contact: Janet McBain (Archivist); Anne Docherty (Administration Officer); Jo Sherington (Librarian)

Collection of non-fiction film 1897-1980s, concerning aspects of Scottish social, cultural and industrial history, on 16mm and 35mm cine film (small holdings on 8mm and 9.5mm), mostly b&w. The collection comprises local cinema newsreels, educational films, documentaries, advertising and promotional films, and amateur footage (the Scottish Film Archive does not hold feature films). Some regional television news, documentary and light entertainment programmes are kept.

Visitors by appointment. Initial written requests for information preferred; write to Administration Officer. Charges made for use of material. NB The Archive cannot offer a hire service on the total collection as viewing/accessible copies are available for only 40% of it. Staff can conduct preliminary research on behalf of enquirers to establish the viability of a visit.

Mon-Fri 0900-1230, 1330-1700.

Film Archive is located next to Notre Dame Primary School in Victoria Crescent Rd (off Byres Rd) 2 miles NW of city centre; Hillhead underground station and bus routes near; limited parking.

Primary source material: Films of Scotland 1954-84, a special collection of approximately 120 titles reflecting aspects of industrial, cultural and public life; small collections of photographs, ephemera and MS relating to cinema exhibition and film production. The Archive is currently computerising records of the collection with a view to publishing a catalogue in the next few years. At present no catalogue exists other than the manual card system on the premises.

Publications: Access charges and conditions of use; Scottish archive film for education (details of video compilations for sale); A4 photocopies of detailed catalogue entries for films in the collection.

192   Scottish Fisheries Museum

St Ayles, Harbourhead, ANSTRUTHER KY10 3AB
Tel.: 0333-310628
Contact: The Manager.

Library (c1000 vols); photographs (c9000) and original documents covering the fishing industry over the last 200 years; with some material relating to Anstruther.

Prior consultation advisable. Annual membership £7.50 or £1.60 daily.

Mon-Sat 1000-1730; Sun 1100-1700 (Apr-Oct); Mon-Sat 1000-1630; Sun 1400-1630 (Nov-Mar).

The Museum is located at east end of Anstruther Harbour; parking opposite; bus stop nearby, disabled access throughout Museum and library, but not to reserve collections or vessels.

Primary source material: Documents covering various aspects of the fishing industry.

Publications: Guide book; general interest leaflet.

Photocopies: A4. Photographs can be ordered.

193   The Scottish Genealogy Society

Library and Family History Centre, 15 Victoria Terrace, EDINBURGH EH1 2JL
Tel.: 031-220 3677   FAX : 0131 220 3677
Contact: The Secretary

The collection is devoted to books on genealogy and family history, including index files on family names; books on topography and emigration from the British Isles to USA, Canada and Australasia; publications of the Scottish History Society and the Scottish Record Society; early runs of the Scots Magazine, Fasti and Scots Peerage, etc.

Prior consultation advisable. Charges: Members free, others £2.00.

Tue 1030-1730; Wed 1430-2030; Sat 1000-1700.

Victoria Terrace is down steps from Johnston Terrace, below Castle, or from George IV Bridge; Waverley railway station 0.5 miles; St Andrew Square Bus Station 0.75 miles; bus routes nearby; parking near; disabled access difficult, enquire in advance.

Primary source material: Census for Edinburgh 1851-61 [mfilm]; IGI(S) to date, with Cumbria and Northumberland, and Ireland; OPRs for Scotland [mfiche]; pre-1855 monumental inscriptions for eleven counties together with others covering the whole of Scotland [MS and printed].

Publications: List of publications issued by the Society; leaflets available to those seeking help with family research; List of professional searchers.

Photocopies: A3, A4. Mfiche prints: A4.

world wide web homepage
http://www.taynet.co.uk/users/scotgensoc
mail scotgensoc@taynet.co.uk

131

194   Scottish Jewish Archives Centre

Garnethill Synagogue, 127 Hill Street, GLASGOW G3 6UB
Contact: Mr Harvey L Kaplan (Director)
Contact's tel.no.: 041-649 4526.

**Wide range of material relating to history of Jewish community
in Scotland, especially Glasgow, Edinburgh, Dundee, Aberdeen,
Ayr, Dunfermline, Greenock, Falkirk & Inverness, late 18thC-.**

Visitors by appointment.

Sun 1400-1600 (once per month).

At the Charing Cross end of Hill St; Queen St & Central railways
stations and bus station 0.75 miles; parking near.

**Primary source material: Minute books of synagogue &
communal organisations; newspapers & newspaper cuttings;
books; photographs of communal buildings, leaders, activities;
papers of communal leaders; financial records & accounts;
annual reports; synagogue registers; brochures & magazines;
year books.**

Reproduction of photographs by arrangement.

195   Scottish Lead Mining Museum

"The Leadminers' Library", Goldscaur Row, WANLOCKHEAD
ML12 6UT
Tel.: 0659-74387
Contact: Ms Joanne Orr

**The miners' library houses a collection of books bought by the
miners 1754-. It is largely theologically-based, plus archives &
village society minute books, mining records and plans.**

Visitors by appointment.

Mon-Fri 0900-1700.

Opposite the Community Centre and war memorial; minimal bus
service; parking nearby; disabled access could be difficult (2 steps).

**Primary source material: Mining company records; maps &
plans; minute books from village band, curling, quoiting
societies; library minute books; photographs and village
memorabilia; village history documented in diaries; Free Church
of Scotland records; miners' bargain records; census returns.**

Publications: The Leadminers' Museum & Wanlockhead; The Leadminers' Library; Catalogue of the book collection (reference only), Catalogue of archives (reference only).

Photocopies: A4.

196   Scottish Library Association

Motherwell Business Centre, Coursington Road, MOTHERWELL ML1 1PW
Tel.: 0698-52526   Fax: 0698-52057
Contact: Mr Robert Craig (Executive Secretary)

The Association maintains SCOTLOC: the Scottish local studies information database, with over 1600 records of publications, in all formats, currently in print and produced by libraries, local history societies, museums, etc; including the catalogue of the Scottish Central Film and Video Library. The package requires a PC-compatible microcomputer with a hard disk; subscriptions are available for corporate or private users.

Publications: Leaflet on SLA publications; Scotland- 1939 / B. Osborne and R. Craig; The coinage of Scotland: a bibliography / P.J. Sweeney; The Glasgow novel: a survey and bibliography / M. Burgess; The Scot and his maps / Margaret Wilkes. 1991; SCOTLOC leaflet.

197   Scottish Maritime Museum

Laird Forge, Gottries Road, IRVINE KA12 8QE
Tel.: 0294-78283
Contact: Mr W Walker (Research Officer)

The Research Department holds a large collection of photographic records of ships which operated to and from Scottish waters (especially the Clyde); also books and archives relating to local shipyards, harbours and shipping activity and some general local themes.

Prior consultation advisable. No admission charge. Search fee at hourly rate.

Mon-Fri 0900-1600.

Off Montgomery Place/Harbour St by Irvine Harbourside; railway station and bus routes near; parking nearby; disabled access possible with assistance.

Primary source material: Nautical magazines 1833-1901; Lloyds Registers 1900-1990 & limited numbers of Lloyd's Registers of yachts; runs of Sea Breezes, Ships Monthly, Yachting Monthly; BSRA reports; transactions of shipbuilders in Scotland; transactions of the Institute of Shipbuilders in the North East, limited lists of ship's movements out of Ayr, Irvine & Troon; documentation on local companies (including the Fairlie Yacht Slip Co. Ltd (Wm Fife & Son), McKnight of Ayr, Ailsa of Troon, Ayrshire Dockyard Co. Ltd of Irvine); Paterson Collection of c23,000 negatives of vessels in Scottish Waters; Scott collection of photographs, press cuttings and ephemera re ships and shipyards.

Photocopies: A3, A4. Availability dependent on condition of original. Photographic service, including drymounting of prints. Price list on request.

198   Scottish Maritime Museum: Denny Ship Model Experiment Tank Archives

Castle Street, DUMBARTON G82 1QS
Tel.: 0389-63444
Contact: Mr Niall MacNeill

A complete record of ship model hull tests conducted 1883-1963 at Denny Ship Model Experiment Tank by Messrs Wm Denny & Bros; data for over 1000 ships built by the firm.

Prior consultation advisable. Charge: 50p if living outside Dumbarton District.

Mon-Sat 1000-1600.

Opposite Safeway supermarket; railway station, bus routes and parking near.

Primary source material: Graphs of hydrodynamic results, lines plans, staff log books, ships specification books, etc., and details of individual research in naval architecture undertaken in the building.

Publications: Denny Tank leaflet.

10x8" photographs of ships by arrangement.

199   Scottish Meteorological Records

The Meteorological Office, Saughton House, Broomhouse Drive,
EDINBURGH EH11 3XQ
Tel.: 031-244 8368   Fax: 031-244 8389
Contact: Mrs E Kerr

**Meteorological records for Scotland dating back to the late
18thC in a variety of MS, charts, tabulations and autographic
records. Data c1960- (earlier for a few locations) also held as
computer records.**

*Visitors by appointment. Charges: free if enquirer willing to do
searches with minimal help.*

Mon-Fri 0900-1600.

3.5 miles west of the city centre; on bus routes; parking; disabled
access.

**Primary source material: Material collected by the Scottish
Meteorological Society in the period 1855-1920 and by the
Meteorological Office 1920-; meteorological records for Scotland
in a variety of MS, charts, tabulation and autographic records
late 18thC-1960; similar material 1960- [MS, computer records
and mfilm].**

Publications: Wide variety of promotional leaflets.

Photocopies: A4.

200   Scottish Mining Museum

Lady Victoria Colliery, NEWTONGRANGE EH22 4QN
Tel.: 031-663 7519
Contact: Mr Mike Ashworth (Curator)

**The Museum Library holds 15000+ books, periodicals, trade
publications and catalogues, maps and associated archive
material covering the technological, social and economic history
of coal, coal mining and the use of coal in Scotland; collections
of photographs, slides and films; and a limited ephemera
collection.**

Visitors by appointment.

Mon-Fri 0930-1630.

The Library is situated in the Visitor Centre of the Museum; Lady Victoria Colliery is on the A7, 10 miles south of Edinburgh; on bus routes; parking; disabled access difficult, contact in advance.

Primary source material: National Coal Board/British Coal Corporation publications including Coal Magazine/Coal News, annual reports & accounts, technical specifications, 1947-; National Union of Mineworkers (Scottish Area) McDonald Memorial Collection including MFGB/NUM annual reports & minutes 1900- [printed] , Scottish executive committee minutes 1945- [printed], closure consultation minutes 1950-70; Royal Commissions on the coal industry 1842-1940; annual reports of the Mines Inspectors (national & divisional) 1900-, Inspectors' incident reports 1920-; reports and publications of the Safety in Mines Research Board 1923-49; reports of the Fuel Research Board 1917-31; Guide to the coalfields 1948-; Colliery Guardian 1949-; Journal of the Institute of Mining Engineers (Federated) 1890-; Colliery Engineering 1924-68; National Association of Colliery Managers Transactions 1909-42; records of the Lothian Coal Company 1890-1947 [MS].

Publications: Library guide leaflet; Wullie Drysdale, a miner & his family 1900; Doos & dugs: miners' pastimes; Serfdom, a species of slave: a short history of coal mining in Scotland; Prestongrange beam engine, a descriptive leaflet.

Photocopies: A3, A4. Limited photography service.

201   Scottish Museums Council: Information Centre

County House, 20-22 Torphichen Street, EDINBURGH EH3 8JB
Tel.: 031-229 7465 Fax: 031-229 2728
Contact: Ms Wilma Alexander (Information Officer)

The Centre holds material on all aspects of Scottish museums, including examples of their information sheets, educational material and details of their collections. It also holds press cuttings and other ephemera relating to Scotland's museums and their history.

Visitors by appointment.

Mon-Fri 0900-1700.

West end of city centre; Haymarket railway station, bus routes and parking nearby; disabled access difficult (unavoidable steps), but prior arrangement possible.

Publications: Scottish Museum News; Museum Abstracts; factsheets and short bibliographies; publications list.

Photocopies: A3, A4.

202 Scottish National Gallery of Modern Art

Belford Road, EDINBURGH EH4 3DR
Tel.: 031-556 8921 x735 Fax: 031-343 2802
Contact: Ms Ann Simpson (Librarian)

Monographs and exhibition catalogues on 20thC painting, sculpture, graphics, etc., including material on Scottish art and artists.

Visitors by appointment.

Mon-Fri 1030-1230, 1330-1630.

1 mile west of Princes St (West End); Haymarket railway station 0.5 miles; on bus route; parking; disabled access.

Primary source material: Artists' letters, photographs, slides, artists' books, sketchbooks; other archival material relating to works in the gallery's collection, much concerning Scottish art & artists.

203 Scottish National Portrait Gallery

1 Queen Street, EDINBURGH EH2 1JD
Tel.: 031-556 8921 x228 Fax: 031-558 3691
Contact: Dr Rosalind K Marshall (Assistant Keeper)

Archive of 30000 b&w photographs of portraits c1550-1991 in other collections in Scotland, England & abroad; 14000 portrait engravings, 2000 portrait drawings; social history index; artists' biographical material. SRA DS 6/17.

Visitors by appointment.

Mon-Sat 1000-1700; Sun 1400-1700.

Near city centre; Waverley railway station 0.5 miles; bus station and off-street parking nearby; on-street parking difficult; disabled access to print room.

Primary source material: c2000 paintings, watercolours, miniature & medallions representing famous Scots from all localities.

Publications: Printed catalogue of the Collection; postcards of some of the paintings.

Photographs 8x6" and larger (b&w). 35mm & 5x4" transparencies (col).

204   The Scottish Natural History Library

Foremount House, KILBARCHAN PA10 2EZ
Tel.: 05057-2419
Contact: Dr J A Gibson (Director)

Largest and most important collection of Scottish natural history books and journals; natural history bibliographical service.

Visitors by appointment.

Kilbarchan Village is 5 miles west of Paisley; bus services to Kilbarchan Village; parking; disabled access.

Primary source material: 100,000 volumes of monographs & journals covering all aspects of natural history in Scotland; publications of local Scottish societies.

Publications: Bibliographical services leaflet.

Photocopies: A3, A4.

205   Scottish Office Libraries: Air Photographs Unit

Room 1/24, New St Andrew's House, EDINBURGH EH1 3SZ
Tel.: 031-244 4263   Fax: 031-244 4785
Contact: Mr Harry Jack (Air Photographs Officer)

Collection of vertical aerial photography covers entire surface of Scotland at 1:10,000 and 1:24,000 scales; many areas at larger scales; all stereoscopic, taken at various dates 1944-. Smaller collection of oblique aerial photography covers most towns and many other areas, mainly late 1940s/early 50s. Index of all known aerial photography of Scotland, giving details (scale, date, source) of available cover.

Visitors by appointment.

Mon-Fri 0900-1630.

East end of Princes St; Waverley railway station, St Andrew Square bus station and parking nearby; disabled access.

Primary source material: Films taken by RAF 1944-, OS 1954-70, and by commercial firms for the Scottish Office at various dates; contact prints 9x9" or smaller, or 16mm mfilm for viewing; mirror stereoscopes available for viewing. NB Because most areas have been photographed on several occasions since 1945 and each photograph is precisely dated, changes in buildings, new construction, demolition and changes in land use can often be dated with greater precision than by maps.

Publications: Information leaflet; price list of photographic services.

Photographs printed to order from films held by the Scottish Office: contact prints, 35mm slides, contact diapositives, enlargements up to 36x36".

206 Scottish Office Libraries: Historic Scotland

20 Brandon Street, EDINBURGH EH3 5DX
Tel.: 031-244 3140   Fax: 031-244 2903
Contact: Mrs Paulette M Hill (Librarian in Charge (Room 369))

Library (Room 369) stock includes reference books; guides to historic buildings and ancient monuments; inventories; official publications; periodicals; Scottish Burgh Surveys; Exploring Scotland's heritage series; Royal Incorporation of Architects of Scotland guides. Subject coverage includes architecture, historic buildings, ancient monuments, archaeology, conservation. Photographs Library (Room 338) has b&w and colour photographs of monuments in care and of listed historic buildings.

Visitors by appointment.

Mon-Fri 0900-1630.

Bottom of Dundas St 0.75 miles north of Princes St; on bus routes; parking by prior arrangement or nearby; disabled access.

Primary source material: Folio works containing architectural drawings.

Publications: Historic Scotland list of and guides to various monuments (available from Room 307).

Photocopies: A4. Mfiche prints: A4. Photographic slides available from Historic Scotland Photographic Library (Room 338).

207   Scottish Office Libraries: New St Andrew's House Library

St James Square, EDINBURGH EH1 3AY
Tel.: 031-244 4799 Fax: 031-244 4785
Contact: The Librarian.

The library holds official reports, etc., produced by the Scottish Office and its predecessors, and reports presented to the Secretary of State by local authorities, etc. Main subjects are public administration, education, planning, economic affairs, transport.

Visitors by appointment.

Mon-Fri 0900-1630.

East end of Princes St; Waverley railway station, bus station and off-street parking nearby; disabled access.

Photocopies: A3, A4. Mfilm/mfiche prints.

208   Scottish Office Libraries: Pentland House Library

Robb's Loan, EDINBURGH EH14 1TW
Tel.: 031-244 6124 Fax: 031-244 6001
Contact: The Librarian.

The library holds official reports, etc., produced by the Scottish Office and its predecessors and reports presented to the Secretary of State by local authorities, etc. Main subjects are agriculture & fisheries administration.

Visitors by appointment.

Mon-Fri 0900-1630.

2 miles south-west of Princes St West End; Haymarket railway station 1.5 miles; bus routes and parking nearby.

Photocopies: A3, A4. Mfilm/mfiche prints.

209   Scottish Office Libraries: St Andrew's House Library

Regent Road, EDINBURGH EH1 3DH
Tel.: 031-244 2619 Fax: 031-244 2683
Contact: The Librarian.

The library holds official reports, etc., produced by the Scottish Office and its predecessors, and reports presented to the Secretary of State by local authorities, etc. Main subjects are public health, social work, police, prisons, housing.

Visitors by appointment.

Mon-Fri 0900-1630.

Eastwards continuation of Princes St; Waverley railway station, bus station and off-street parking near; disabled access.

Photocopies: A3, A4. Mfilm/mfiche prints.

210   Scottish Record Office 0131-535-1314

General Register House, Princes Street, EDINBURGH EH1 3YY
Tel.: 031-556 6585 ~~344~~ ~~430 51 1414~~ 314 -445 1

NEW REGISTER HOUSE - 0131-535-1414

SRO contains the widest ranging archive holdings in Scotland; government and legal records; many private and local records; an extensive collection of maps and estate plans. Holdings date from the 12thC, the bulk of the material dating from the 16th century. A small specialised library containing historical, biographical, legal and topographical works may be consulted by readers. Full internal, and a number of published, catalogues and guides to the various record groups may be consulted.

Enquiries should be directed to the Keeper of the Records. Visitors should check in advance which Search Room (see below) holds the records they wish to consult; this may be done by telephone unless enquiry is an involved one.

Mon-Fri 0900-1645 (groups by arrangement).

There are two Search Rooms: Historical Search Room at HM General Register House: east end of Princes St opposite North Bridge; St Andrew Square bus station, Waverley railway station and parking nearby; disabled access. West Search Room in West Register House: west side of Charlotte Square; St Andrew Square bus station 0.75 miles; Haymarket railway station 0.5 miles; on-street parking; off-street parking near; disabled access.

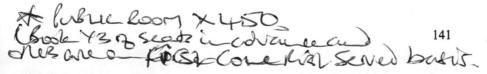

Public Room X 450
(Book X3 of seats in advance a)
others are on first come first served basis.

Primary source material: Public legal registers (deeds & sasines); Court of Session, High Court of Justiciary and Sheriff Court records; Commissary Court records (NB testaments); Kirk Session and presbytery records, Church of Scotland and other Presbyterian groups records with several deposits from other denominations; valuation rolls (complete); heritors records (information on schools, manses, roads, etc.); Exchequer records including taxation schedules, customs accounts, Forfeited Estate papers; Customs & Excise records; records of National Coal Board and British Railways Board, Scottish areas, with earlier constituent companies; family papers; commercial and industrial firms' records; Register House Plans series; Departmental files of modern government containing information on many local topics, last quarter of the 19thC- (subject to the 30 year closure rule).

Publications: Holdings and services; Maritime and railway history; Plans; Family and local history sources; Edinburgh; Archives in school; A guide for students; A short guide to the records (leaflet 7); SRO publications (leaflet 15); Tracing your Scottish ancestors. - 1991.

Photocopies: A2, A3, A4. Film prints: A1, A2, A3, A4. Mfilm/mfiche copies: details on request. Documents must be readily identified if ordering copies by post and must be prepaid.

211   Shetland Archives

44 King Harald Street, LERWICK ZE1 0EQ
Tel.: 0595-3535 x269 Fax: 0595-2810
Contact: Mr Brian Smith

The Shetland Archives contain local authority record collections, plus Crown records held under charge and superintendence of the Keeper of Records of Scotland; miscellaneous gifts of private records; oral history material from throughout Shetland; and printed local history material.

Visitors by appointment.

Mon-Thu 0900-1300, 1400-1700; Fri 0900-1300, 1400-1600.

In centre of Lerwick; limited parking; disabled access.

Primary source material: OPRs and censuses for all Shetland; registers of sasines to 1781 and abridgments thereafter; testaments, etc., [mfilm].

Photocopies: A3, A4.

212   **Shetland Library**

Lower Hillhead, LERWICK ZE1 0EL
Tel.: 0595-3868
Contact: Mr John G Hunter (Chief Librarian)

Collection of Shetlandiana including books, pamphlets, photos, postcards, newspaper clippings, newspapers.

Prior consultation advisable.

Mon, Wed, Fri 1000-1900; Tue, Thu, Sat 1000-1700.

In town centre near Town Hall; on-street parking.

Primary source material: The Shetland News 1886-1962, The Shetland Times 1872- [mfilm] (both being indexed).

Photocopies: A4.

213   **Shetland Museum**

Lower Hillhead, LERWICK ZE1 0EL
Tel.: 0595-5057
Contact: Mr Tommy Watt (Curator)

Extensive photographic library (collection catalogued).

Mon, Wed, Fri 1000-1900; Tue, Thu, Sat 1000-1700.

In town centre near Town Hall; on-street parking; disabled access with stairlift; elevating wheelchair available.

Primary source material: Archive material covers the museum's own collections.

Photocopies: A3, A4. Photographs supplied by arrangement.

214   **Signet Library**

Parliament Square, EDINBURGH EH1 1RF
Tel.: 031-225 4923   Fax: 031-220 4016
Contact: The Librarian.

The Library contains a Scottish section of c20000 vols that includes many titles relating to local history throughout the country. It does not specialise in a particular area or subject.

Visitors by appointment.

Mon-Fri 0930-1600.

Off High St (Royal Mile) beside St Giles Cathedral & court buildings; Waverley railway station 0.25 miles; St Andrew Square bus station 0.5 miles; on bus routes; parking nearby.

Primary source material: Printed Session Papers collection of 700 vols covering 1713-1820, concerning Scottish civil cases heard in the Court of Session, many containing information relating to local disputes, etc., often in some detail (although couched in legal language, they can provide data not available elsewhere; the Papers are indexed by subject, and by the parties involved in the case, making the set unique).

Photocopies: A3, A4.

215   Springburn Museum Trust

Atlas Square, Ayr Street, GLASGOW G21 4BW
Tel.: 041-557 1405
Contact: Alison Cutforth (Curator); Eileen Gordon (Outreach Officer)

Social history and photographic collections include a large section on the railway companies of Springburn; and part of the John Thomas Collection.

Visitors by appointment if specialist information required.

Mon-Fri 1030-1700; Sat 1000-1630; Sun, Bank Holidays 1400-1700.

1.75 miles north of city centre next to Springburn railway station; on bus routes; parking; disabled access.

Publications: The Springburn experience: an oral history of work in a railway community from 1840 / G. Hutchison & M. O'Neill; Glasgow: locomotive builder to the world / M. Nicholson & M. O'Neill; Up oor close / Jean Faley; publication list.

Photographic copy service.

216 **St Andrews University Library: Manuscripts & Muniments Department**

North Street, ST ANDREWS KY16 9TR
Tel.: 0334-76161 x514
Contact: Mr R N Smart (Keeper of Manuscripts and University Muniments)

A special St Andrews collection of printed materials has a particular emphasis on works about the town and university. The general collection of printed books contains many works of interest to the local historian both of Fife and elsewhere in Scotland. An extensive collection of MS, archives and photographs has a clear bias towards the North of Fife, but some material is of relevance to other areas. SRA DS 6/23.

Prior consultation advisable.

Mon-Fri 0900-1300, 1400-1700; Sat (term) 0900-1200.

University Library building in North St is one block west of St Salvators College tower; bus station near; Leuchars railway station 4 miles (bus or taxi); on-street parking; disabled access from The Scores.

Primary source material: Estate and family papers, business records, maps and architectural plans, etc., mainly concerning North East Fife; St Andrews University's own records including property administration papers 1413- (with some earlier charters); burgh records of North East Fife District (Anstruther, Auchtermuchty, Crail, Cupar, Earlsferry, Elie, Falkland, Kilrenny, Ladybank, Newburgh, Newport, Pittenweem, St Andrews, St Monance, and Tayport); church records of congregations in the former presbyteries of Cupar and St Andrews and of the presbyteries themselves; photographic collections including Valentine & Sons Ltd (157000 items) covering the whole of the British Isles, George Cowie (99000) covering North East Fife; Robert M. Adam (14000) covering Scottish topography (especially the Highlands), and some dozen other smaller collections.

Publications: Manuscripts and Muniments Department leaflet.

Photocopies: A3, A4. Prints from film 7x5"-20x16" (b&w, col). Slides.

217   Stevenson College: Library

Bankhead Avenue, EDINBURGH EH11 4DE
Tel.: 031-453 6161 x212   Fax: 031-458 5067
Contact: College Librarian.

Collection includes Robert Stevenson (lighthouse engineer)
1772-1850; Life of Robert Stevenson / David Stevenson; Records
of a family of engineers / Robert Louis Stevenson; Biographical
sketch of the late Robert Stevenson / Alan Stevenson; The Bell
Rock lighthouse: passages selected from an account of the Bell
Rock lighthouse / edited by A.F. Collins; plus several modern
monographs on the history of lighthouses; some aerial
photographs & postcards of Stevenson lighthouses.

Visitors by appointment.

Mon, Fri 0845-1645; Tue-Thu 0845-1920 (term); Mon-Fri
1000-1600 (vacation).

4 miles west of city centre; bus routes nearby; parking; disabled
access.

Primary source material: One vol of Robert Stevenson's Journal
1801-1818 [MS]; copies of three letters.

Publications: Robert Stevenson 1772-1850 (leaflet).

Photocopies: A4.

218   Stewarton & District Museum

District Council Office, Avenue Square, STEWARTON KA3 5AP
Contact: Mr A Gourley (Trustee); Mr I H MacDonald (Chairman
of Museum Trustees)
Contacts' tel.nos.: 0560-84249 (Trustee); 0563-24748 (Chairman).

A small library of reference books; albums of old photographs;
tapes of interviews with local people; assorted document
extracts.

Visitors by appointment.

In town centre; railway station 0.25 miles; bus routes nearby;
parking.

Primary source material: Census 1841-51-61 [mfilm]; OPRs [mfilm]; gravestone records with indexes; Bonnet court transactions (extracts); Baron court records.

Photographs supplied by arrangement.

219 Stewartry Museum

St Mary Street, KIRKCUDBRIGHT DG6 4AQ
Tel.: 0557-31643
Contact: Dr D F Devereux (Museum Curator)

The museum holds a general library relating to the history of Galloway and the Stewartry plus archive and photographic collections covering the Stewartry.

Visitors by appointment.

Mon-Fri 0900-1300, 1400-1700.

In town centre at the south end of St Mary St; parking; bus routes nearby; disabled access possible with assistance.

Primary source material: Kirkcudbright Town Council minutes 1576-1870 [MS & printed] and miscellaneous burgh archives 1680-; miscellaneous burgh archives from Castle Douglas, Gatehouse-of-Fleet, New Galloway 1785- [MS]; papers of Kirkcudbright Gentlemen and Yeomanry Cavalry 1804-36, and Independent Kirkcudbright Troop of Yeomanry Cavalry 1831-36 [MS]; miscellaneous collection of archives, maps, plans, photographs relating to Kirkcudbright and the Stewartry.

Photocopies: A3, A4.

220 Stirling District Libraries

Central Library, Corn Exchange Road, STIRLING FK8 2HX
Tel.: 0786-71293   Fax: 0786-73094
Contact: Mr Allan Jeffrey

The local history collection includes works about Central Region and to some extent by local authors, local newspapers, miscellaneous maps, photographs and ephemera. Indexes available for Stirling Journal 1820-1970 and Stirling Observer 1836-56.

Prior consultation advisable.

Mon, Wed, Fri-Sat 0930-1700; Tue, Thu 0930-1900.

In town centre; railway, bus stations and parking near; limited access for disabled (flight of stairs).

Primary source material: Stirling Journal and Advertiser 1820-June 1970 [printed & mfilm]; Stirling Observer June 1970- [printed & mfilm]; Stirling Sentinel Oct 1889-Nov 1907 [printed]; Stirling Sentinel miscellaneous vols 1929-57; Bridge of Allan Gazette 1884-1971 [printed]; Callander Advertiser 1884-1971 [printed]; Scottish Record Society publications including Commissariot Record of Stirling Register of Testaments 1607-1800 index [printed], Commissariot Record of Dunblane Register of Testaments 1539-1900 index [printed]; Scottish History Society series 1-5 [printed]; census enumeration books 1841-81 Stirlingshire [mfilm]; census enumeration books 1841-51 Perthshire [mfilm]; IGI(GB) [mfilm].

Photocopies: A3, A4. Fax machine for public use.

221   **Stirling University: Library**

STIRLING FK9 4LA
Tel.: 0786-73171   Fax: 0786-63000
Contact: Ms Caroline Rowlinson (Grierson Archive); Mr Gordon Willis (Other collections)
Contacts' tel.nos.: 0786-67228 (Grierson Archive), 0786-67236 (other collections).

Printed books on local history are in the general history collection. The special collections contain MS & printed material on a number of specific topics, including newspapers.

Visitors by appointment for special collections.

Mon-Fri 0900-2200, Sat 0930-1230, Sun 1400-2100 (term), Mon-Fri 0900-1700 (vacation).

University is situated on the A9, on the outskirts of Bridge of Allan; bus service to library entrance from Stirling bus and railway stations and Bridge of Allan railway station; parking; disabled access.

Primary source material: Grierson Archive, correspondence & papers of John Grierson, founder of the documentary film movement; Letterbooks, accounts, etc. of Howietoun Fishery 1873-1978; MS records, including registers of borrowings, of the Leighton Library, Dunblane (founded 1687); Tait Collection (socialist material) including correspondence, minute books, etc., of left-wing political parties, mainly in Edinburgh 1883-1943; Drummond Collection of publications of the Drummond Press/Stirling Tract Enterprise 1848-1980; Stirling Journal & Advertiser 1820-1970 [mfilm] (except 1960-1964); Stirling

Observer 1971- [mfilm]; Devon-Valley Tribune 1899-1953 [mfilm], 1953-1967 [printed].

Publications: Special Collections leaflet; Stirling Journal & Advertiser: a local index 1820-1970 (3 vols); John Grierson Archive: list of contents; Leighton Library, Dunblane: catalogue of MS; Leighton Library, Dunblane: its history and contents; Stirling Tract Enterprise and the Drummonds.

Photocopies: A3, A4. Mfilm/mfiche prints: A4.

222   **Strathclyde Regional Archives**

Mitchell Library, North Street, GLASGOW G3 7DN
Tel.: 041-227 2405 0141-287-2999
Contact: Mr A M Jackson (Principal Archivist)
Contacts' tel.nos.: 041-227 2401 (Principal Archivist), 2404 (Searchroom Archivist).

Local authority archives within Strathclyde Region, excluding most burgh and district councils and the former county of Argyll; and a wide range of family, estate, business and church records. There is a small reference library of books on archival subjects and local history. SRA DS 6/11.

Prior consultation advisable. No charge for normal historical enquiries.

Mon-Thu   0930-1645;   Fri   0930-1600   (other   times   by arrangement).

The Mitchell Library is 0.75 miles west of city centre beside the motorway; Central & Queen St railway stations & bus station 0.75 miles; Charing X railway station & bus routes nearby; parking in the surrounding area is difficult; access for disabled should be arranged in advance of visit.

Primary source material: Archives of Glasgow Corporation and the former county councils within Strathclyde (except Argyll) [mainly MS]; the family papers of the Colquhouns of Luss, Maxwells of Pollok, Stirlings of Keir and others; business records including those of several shipyards and engineering firms; church records, maps, plans and photographs; and the modern records of Strathclyde Regional Council.

Publications: General leaflets on the office and the Ayr sub-office; and a leaflet with advice for genealogists; Old Glasgow streets / R. Kenna. - 1990.

Photocopies: A3, A4. Photographic services can be arranged.

223   Strathclyde University: Andersonian Library

Curran Building, 101 St James Road, GLASGOW G4 0NS
Tel.: 041-552 3701 x4135   Fax: 041-552 3304
Contact: Mr J M Allan (Sub-Librarian Special Collections Section)

Selection of secondary, with some primary, material on Glasgow and Scottish economic and social history, with an emphasis on the 19thC. SRA DS 6/13.

Prior consultation advisable. Charges on request.

Mon-Fri 0900-2100 (term); Mon-Fri 0900-1700 (vacations).

The Andersonian Library is near the city centre between Cathedral St & St James' Rd; Queen St railway station nearby; Central railway station 0.75 miles; bus station near; bus routes nearby; limited street parking; access for disabled at St James' Rd entrance.

Primary source material: Glasgow Stock Exchange Daily Lists 1847-1963 [printed]; notebooks of Professor John Anderson (1726-96), founder of University of Strathclyde [MS]; Ludovic Kennedy's papers on the Meehan case [MS & printed] (restricted access); publications from Guy A. Aldred's presses [printed]; Glasgow Dilettante Society Exhibition Books [printed]; selection of source material on Glasgow and region in Robertson and other Collections [printed].

Photocopies: A3, A4. Mfiche/mfilm prints: A4. Photographic services by arrangement.

224   Strathkelvin District Libraries: Reference & Local History Section

The William Patrick Library, Camphill Avenue, KIRKINTILLOCH G66 1DW
Tel.: 041-776 1328   Fax: 041-776 1328
Contact: Mr D Martin; Mrs C Miller

A local studies collection with 1200+ books and pamphlets (mostly dealing with Strathkelvin, but also covering adjacent areas); comprehensive collection of OS and other maps of Strathkelvin; 20000+ photographs, mostly with negatives, and a similar number of 35mm transparencies; OPRs and census returns 1841-1881 for the parishes of Cadder, Kirkintilloch, Baldernock & Campsie; file of Kirkintilloch Herald 1940-; Kirkintilloch Herald 1886-1974 [mfilm]; Kirkintilloch Gazette 1898-1938 [mfilm]; short runs of various other local newspapers, including Bishopbriggs papers.

Prior consultation advisable.

Mon-Tue, Thu-Fri 0930-2000; Wed 0930-1300, 1400-1700; Sat 0930-1300.

The William Patrick Library is near the town centre; access by path through the Peel Park; or by car via Camphill Ave; bus services near; limited parking.

Primary source material: Archives of Burghs of Bishopbriggs and Kirkintilloch; personal papers of Provost James Peter of Kirkintilloch (which usefully supplement the official archives); archives of numerous local societies & community groups (especially from Kirkintilloch, Lenzie, Lennoxtown, Milton of Campsie, Chryston & Stepps); family papers of the Cleland family of Chryston; papers of local historian John Cameron (Campsie & Kirkintilloch); archives of the Lion Foundry, Kirkintilloch (catalogue, photogrpahs, drawings, etc.); documentary material relating to the other local firms, to local railways, and to the Forth & Clyde Canal; papers of Peter Mackenzie, Glasgow Historian, especially relating to radical activity during the late 18th & early 19thC.

Publications: Local publications and local history services leaflets.

Photocopies: A3, A4. 10x8" copy prints of most photographs in the collection.

225   Strathkelvin District Museums

The Cross, KIRKINTILLOCH G66 1AB
Tel.: 041-775 1185
Contact: The Curator.

Collection of local photographs and ephemera.

Prior consultation advisable.

Tue-Fri 1000-1200, 1400-1700.

Museum is at the top of Main St; bus routes nearby; parking.

Primary source material: Comprehensive collection of iron foundry patterns, photographs & some records relating to Lion Foundry; photographic collection of local industries, local personalities & local life; good local postcard collection.

Publications: 30 information sheets on local history topics.

Photocopies: A3, A4.

226   Summerlee Heritage Trust: Museum

West Canal Street, COATBRIDGE ML5 1QD
Tel.: 0236-31261   Fax: 0236-40429
Contact: Ms Carol Haddow (Curator); Mr Frank Little (Curator)

Local history collection of photographs, catalogue & papers relating to Monklands District; particular emphasis is placed on industrial records. There are local plans and maps mainly 19th & 20thC; plus a reference library of books, mainly industrial history.

Sun-Sat 1000-1700.

Near town centre; railway stations and bus routes near; parking; disabled access.

Photocopies: A3, A4. Prints from photographs can be arranged.

227   Sunart Archive

The Old Manse, STRONTIAN PH36 4JB
Tel.: 0967-2149
Contact: Mr George P Fox

Local history material on Ardnamurchan including postcards (local & Western Highlands); photographs, books, plans, maps and newspaper cuttings.

Visitors by appointment. No fee for admission. Search charges negotiable.

1 mile north of village centre on Polloch Rd.

Primary source material: Photographic survey of Ardnamurchan.

Publications: The Floating Church / George P. Fox.

Photocopies: A4.

228   **Tayside Health Board**

PO Box 75, Vernonholme, Riverside Drive, DUNDEE DD1 9NL
Tel.: 0382-645151   Fax: 0382-69734
Contact: Mr James Mair (Press & Public Relations Officer)

**Records of the hospitals in the Tayside Health Board area are
kept in a variety of locations: the majority of records for
Dundee are in the University of Dundee Archives Department,
but some items are in the care of the Archives Centre of Dundee
(contact Mr Ian Flett, tel.no.: (00382-23141), whilst the sederunt
minute books of Dundee Royal Infirmary 1793-1948 are in the
Archive of St Andrews University. A similar situation applies
to hospitals in the Angus, Perth and Kinross areas. Enquirers
should contact the Press and Public Relations Officer for further
information.**

229   **Tweeddale Museum**

Chambers Institute, High Street, PEEBLES EH45 8AP
Tel.: 0721-20123   Fax: 0721-20620
Contact: Ms Rosemary Hanney

**Newspaper cuttings; legal & business documents relating to
Peebles; 200+ photographs, mostly early 20thC; portraits of
local people.**

Prior consultation advisable.

**Mon-Fri 1000-1300, 1400-1700 (Nov-Easter); Mon-Fri 1000-1300,
1400-1700, Sat-Sun 1400-1700 (Easter-Oct).**

In centre of town; on bus routes; parking nearby; disabled access
difficult, prior contact advisable.

Photocopies can be arranged.

230   **Uig Historical Society**

Lochcroistean Centre, UIG, ISLE OF LEWIS PA86 9EP
Tel.: 0851-75456

**Miscellaneous papers; collection of 800 photographs 1880-1940;
crofting history of West Uig in map form.**

*Prior consultation advisable. Visitors by appointment outwith
opening hours.*

Mon-Fri 1400-1600 (Jun-Sep).

Lochcroistean Centre is on the B8011 Garynahine to Timsgarry road; on bus route, limited service; parking.

Publications: World War II Roll of Honour.

231 W H Welsh Educational & Historic Trust

c/o Bridge of Allan Library, Fountain Road, BRIDGE OF ALLAN FK9 4AT
Tel.: 0786-833680
Contact: The Librarian, or members of the Trust and Local History Group.

Books, photographs and local history material for Bridge of Allan and parishes of Lecropt and Logie; mostly Victorian and Edwardian photographs relating to the Spa.

Visitors by appointment, especially if seeking contact with a member of the Trust or Local History Group.

Mon, Fri 0900-1300, 1400-1700; Tue, Thu 0900-1300, 1400-1900; Sat 0900-1200.

Library is in the town centre off Henderson St; bus routes & parking nearby; disabled access.

Primary source material: Memoirs of Dr Welsh.

Publications: Bridge of Allan, in pictures.

Photocopies: A3, A4.

232 West Highland Museum

Cameron Square, FORT WILLIAM PH33 6AJ
Tel.: 0397-702169
Contact: Ms Fiona C Marwick (Curator)

Small varied collection of 18th & 19thC papers.

Prior consultation advisable.

Mon-Fri 1000-1300, 1400-1700.

Central square off the High St; railway & bus stations 0.5 miles; parking nearby.

Primary source material: Papers covering the military occupation and the '45; accounts & minute books of various local committees.

233 West Lothian District Libraries: Local History Collection

Wellpark, Marjoribanks Street, BATHGATE EH48 1AN
Tel.: 0506-52866 x21
Contact: Miss Sybil Calderwood

A collection of books, articles, photographs, slides, maps, videos, newspapers & ephemera about West Lothian, and a small collection of books by West Lothian authors.

Mon, Wed-Thu 0830-1700; Tue 0830-1930; Fri 0830-1600; Sat (1st & 3rd of month) 0900-1300.

Near centre of town; bus routes near; parking.

Primary source material: Lothian Courier 1873-, Linlithgow Journal & Gazette 1891-, Midlothian Advertiser 1906-67 [mfilm]; censuses 1841-81 [mfilm]; OPRs [mfilm]; IGI(S,I) [mfiche]; minutes of Old Burgh and District Councils, West Lothian County and District minutes and Lothian Region minutes; miscellaneous archival records.

Publications: Local History Collection leaflet describing holdings; Digging up your family tree; reproductions of old photographs of West Lothian; A history of the town and Palace of Linlithgow (1879) / G. Waldie (reprint).

Photocopies: A3, A4. Mfilm prints.

234 West Lothian History & Amenity Society Library

c/o West Lothian District Library, Linlithgow Branch, Vennel, LINLITHGOW EH49 7EX
Contact: Mrs Mary Thomson; Mrs P Crichton
Contacts' tel.nos.: 0506-842526 (Mrs Thomson, Linlithgow), 0506-890213 (Mrs Crichton, Winchburgh).

Books about West Lothian topography, geology, industrial history.

Mon-Fri 0900-1700.

Library is in the centre of the town; bus routes nearby; parking; disabled access.

Primary source material: Unbound archival material including photographs, pamphlets, etc., kept by Mrs Crichton at her home (details on request).

Publications: Library catalogue and publications list.

235   Western Isles Libraries: Community Library

Castlebay Community School, CASTLEBAY, ISLE OF BARRA PA80 5XD
Tel.: 08714-471   Fax: 08714-650
Contact: Ms Linda Mackinnon

The small local history and Gaelic collection contains books, articles, maps & some periodicals.

Mon, Wed 0900-1630; Tue, Thu 0900-1630, 1800-2000; Fri 0900-1500; Sat 1000-1230.

The library is within the School; parking; disabled access.

236   Western Isles Libraries: Community Library

Sgoil Lionacleit, LINICLATE, ISLE OF BENBECULA PA88 5PJ
Tel.: 0870-2211 x126   Fax: 0870-2817
Contact: Ms Janet Doe
Faxes should be marked FAO Library.

The Local History and Gaelic Reference collections contain a growing collection of books, articles, periodicals & maps.

Mon, Wed-Thu 0900-1600; Tue, Fri 0900-2000; Sat 1100-1300, 1400-1600.

The Library is situated adjacent to the museum in the Community School at Liniclate; limited public transport; parking; disabled access.

Primary source material: Census 1841-1881 (Uists & Barra) [mfilm]; OPRs 1800-1850 [mfilm]; school log books (closed schools in Uists) 1870s-1980s (gaps).

Photocopies: A3, A4.

237 Western Isles Libraries: Public Library

Keith Street, STORNOWAY, ISLE OF LEWIS PA87 2QG
Tel.: 0851-3064 Fax: 0851-5657
Contact: Mr Robert M Eaves

The local history and Gaelic reference room has a comprehensive collection of books, articles, periodicals, maps, photographs, etc.

Prior consultation advisable.

Mon-Thu 1000-1700; Fri 1000-1900; Sat 1000-1300.

Close to the town centre at the junction of James St & Keith St; bus station & parking near; limited parking at library; disabled access possible.

Primary source material: Census 1841-1881 for Western Isles [mfilm]; OPRs 1800-1850 [mfilm]; school log books (closed schools) 1870s-1980s (gaps); estate rent rolls 1860s-1930s (gaps) [some photocopies]; Stornoway Gazette 1917- [mfilm]; West Highland Free Press 1972- [mfilm]; aircraft movement log books 1963-1985; air traffic control watch log 1963-1985; miscellaneous collection of MS papers of local authors.

Photocopies: A3, A4. Mfilm/fiche prints: A4.

238   Wigtown District Museum Service: District Archive

Stranraer Museum, 55 George Street, STRANRAER DG9 7JP
Tel.: 0776-5088   Fax: 0776-4819
Contact: Ms Alison G Reid (Curator); Mr N Hunter (Museum Assistant)

District Archive includes material dating back to the late 1500s. Photographic collection includes some original works, and many copy negatives.

Visitors by appointment.

Mon-Sat 1000-1700.

The museum is on the corner of George St & Church St; on bus routes; parking nearby; disabled access.

Primary source material: The historic archive covering the four burghs of the district, Stranraer, Newton Stewart, Whithorn and Wigtown, dating back to the late 1500s in some cases; in addition there are some archives relating to Wigtown County and specific groups such as the Commissioners of Police, treasurers accounts and the workings of the Rhins and Machars Councils; there are also archives relating to businesses including protocol books of the early 1600s and individual records.

Publications: General leaflet; Wigtown walks; The textile industry in Wigtownshire.

Photocopies: A2, A3, A4. Photographic service available.

INDEX OF PLACES

Placenames in this index refer to the locations of organisations and resource centres. The numbers in bold refer to Directory entry numbers, not page numbers.